# THE
# ONE
# MINUTE
# DOG TRAINER

**By: Donna Marie Casey**

ISBN-13: 978-1979921428

ISBN-10: 1979921423

# Table of Contents

## Dedication:

This book is dedicated to my beloved sister **Francine Sheila Casey**. *She was not only my sister, she was my best friend... A devoted & amazing, single mother of two beautiful girls, Stephanie & Casey. A loving & supportive daughter, the greatest "baby sister" to a family of 4 girls & no doubt the "coolest" Aunt any child could want. Francine was full of laughter, love & fun. She was the comedian in our family. She possessed an undying love for <u>all</u> animals. As children we would jokingly call her Dr. Doolittle as every injured or distressed animal she came in contact with, she would bring home. Francine brought home countless numbers of stray dogs & cats, she even raised baby chicks. From wild birds to butterflies, Francine would nurse them back to health, then set them free. She gave me the vision &inspiration to write this book. She was the most extraordinary person and many others I have ever known. Although Francine is no longer with us, she is always in our hearts. She still remains my inspiration & encouragement.*

# "Francine & Theo"

# *Acknowledgements:*

I would like to acknowledge a special person in my life to whom I owe a debt of appreciation & gratitude. It would be difficult to express in words, how this person has made and continues to make an extraordinary impact my life. Without this man, my canine knowledge, training career and this book would not have been conceivable. Throughout our many years of friendship, he has signified countless things to me. He was and remains my mentor, the brother I never had, a life coach & mentor to my son, he continues to be an honest & true advisor both in business and in my personal life. More importantly, he is a trusted, loyal & true friend. His name is **Ross Coleman**. I want to thank him for being in my life. There is much love here for him.

An exceptional thank you to my son, **Thomas F. Lane.** Thomas stood by me, throughout his adolescent years, & made numerous sacrifices without which, my career as a Professional Canine Trainer may not have been possible. Thomas trusted me & in my ability to keep "our" lives moving forward, no matter what! He stood by me & believed in me. He will forever have my unconditional love.

Countless thanks to all of my family, especially my mother **Francine DeSantis** , my sister **Paula Jacobs-Beck** , my aunt **Cathleen Cannata** and **all of my nieces & nephews,** without who's reassurance, endless love & support I would not have been able to move ahead with my dreams.

# Acknowledgements:

An extraordinary world of thanks to **Dr. Alexis Baffa,** a very dear friend & has been for years. She is not only the veterinarian to many of my client's canines, she is also the veterinarian to own Bichon Frise', "Buddy". Alexis Baffa is one of the most exceptional people I have ever known. She not only treats puppies, dogs, kittens & cats but also has a unique ability to treat exotic animals. She possesses a devotion, love & dedication for "all animals". Her presence in my life has not only been a personal inspiration but also a true professional inspiration. She is like a sister to me. Alexis is one of the most dedicated veterinarian's in the industry today. She treats her clients (and their animals) with love, honesty, respect & dignity to which I hold with the highest regard. Alexis also runs a private rescue for puppies, dogs, kittens & cats who are in need of a forever home. Many times fostering these animals in need in her own home.

**Donna – Buddy – Elli – Alexis**

**Elli**

Alexis & I not only share a very amazing friendship, we also share a special & loving bond with an astonishing **German Shepard, her name is Elli.** I met & trained Ellie at the age of 9 weeks old. Elli & I "imprinted" immediately. We shared a distinctive connection from the day we met. Through an unfortunate circumstance, Elli had to be surrendered by her previous owner. Her previous owner, had developed a medical condition shortly after I completed basic obedience training with her. His condition would prevent him from keeping her. He called me & shared his unfortunate experience. He was devastated and so was I, however he knew the love Elli & I shared was special and therefore there was only one solution, I would personally take Elli to be my own. There was just no way I could say no. I was unable to take Elli immediately so I asked Alexis to foster her for me. She gladly agreed and took Elli home with her that very night. Soon after, Alexis fell in love with Elli. Today Elli lives with Dr. Alexis Baffa & her "pack" which includes (at least for today) 6 dogs, 7 cats & a bird. After Alexis & I mutually decided that Elli was a great fit for her pack, we went on to train Ellie to be a Certified Service Animal. Together we worked diligently to train Elli, what we consider to be, "**The Ideal Service Animal**".

# Acknowledgements:

**To the myriad of Client (Canine Parents)** - I cannot thank you enough! For over the years, you have welcomed me into your homes, trusted my canine training abilities and provided me with the <u>**privilege**</u> & <u>**luxury**</u> of working with you, your families, & your endearing pets. Each of you have forever changed & enriched my life. Many of the photos in this book are of my client's loving pets. Because of my love for each and every one of them, the photos appearing in this book were <u>chosen by a "neutral subeditor"</u> as it would have been impossible for me to choose. I truly love them all.

**To all of my endearing friends, colleagues & associates.** There are simply too many of you to mention by name. You know who you are! You have been my cheer leaders, and provided me with so much encouragement. I love you all!

A very special thanks to **Eileen Higgins** from "**Dream in Color Photography**". She is one of the most gifted Professional Photographers I know. She created the cover photographs & many other photos that appear in this book. She did an amazing job!

I cannot forget my dear friend "**Annemarie**" who assisted the photography coordination efforts with Eileen Higgins during the photo shoot. Annemarie was unbelievable! She took control, directing me, my numerous clients and their canines. Thank you both so very much! You are amazing to work with.

Special thanks to my dear friend Matthew Tsombanis who helped me put this book together and get it off the ground! I could not have done it without you!

# *Introduction*
## *About "THE" dog trainer*

"THE" dog trainer, better known as **Donna Marie Casey**. Originally born in Wyckoff Heights, Brooklyn NY. Raised in Queens NY, until I became a young adult then later moved to Long Island New York.

I have always had a very special connection with animals, especially canines. When I was growing up, we owned countless numbers of puppies & dogs. My youngest sister, Francine & I usually took the initiative when it came to training our pets. It just came natural to us.

After graduating High School, I took a few college courses, then decided to go to work full time in the Telecommunications (Telecom) Voice and Data Services Industry. It was an "up & coming" industry otherwise known as a "White Collar" world. The Telecom industry was considered to be, back in the day, a "man's profession". Yet there I was a young woman, working in a man's world, talk about challenging. I was young & talented and wanted to make a name for myself in the industry.

When I began working in the Telecom Industry, "The Phone Company" had a monopoly on voice and data services. The Telecom Industry was on the brink of becoming a very competitive world. In 1982 "Divestiture" of "The Phone Company" became a reality. It was "A Time of Change". After "divestiture" the Telecom Industry exploded. I was in the right place at the right time.

## About "THE" dog trainer

My Telecom career was scoring however I still possessed this undying desire to work with canines. I volunteered at a few rescues and shelters for a time, however, it didn't seem to be enough. As life would have it, that is when I first met Ross Coleman. Today he still one of my dearest friends. Ross took me under his wing, mentored me, and taught me the secrets of successful business and the profound success of canine training. In June of 1986, I became a Certified Master Canine Trainer.

I was training canines - here and there – one would say, for me, canine training was a part time gig. I was mainly canine training just for the love of it. It was gratifying to me & I was able to change people's lives, one puppy/one dog at a time. However, I was also quite content earning (what would later become) a "six figure income" in the Telecom Industry. I was torn between both worlds. I wanted to continue to train canines however it was an easy decision to follow the money. I stayed in the Telecom Industry for many years. Time moved on and I became a single mother. Talk about a life changer!

Once a single mother, the importance of establishing myself in the Telecom Industry became even more essential to my life. It seemed to be "the next right thing" to do. I was, back in the day, what people would call a "control freak". I had my life all planned out. "Life according to Donna" I would jokingly say. I was to have the comfort of a, guaranteed and growing income with a solid & upcoming company in an industry that was booming yet I could train canines just for the love of it. I thought I had found my life's purpose. I changed companies & positions once the "The Phone Company" divested. I moved around in the Telecom Industry for a while. Eventually I took a position in a well-known & well established "Utility Company" on Long Island. The company was just beginning to spread its wings into data & voice services. It was a very exciting time. I was hired as a Senior Sales Manager. New sales were pouring in. The company was beginning to build fiber networks all over Long Island. After several months, the company began building new fiber networks throughout the Tristate area.

New voice and data business clients were jumping on the band wagon, not only to save money, but to receive enhanced, leading edge technology for their voice and data services. As time passed I continued training canines, I view training as a hobby. It was a love that I could continue, while climbing the preverbal white collar corporate ladder.

At the same time, through word of mouth, more & more new 'canine parents" began to requesting me to train their pups. I was becoming increasingly more popular on Long Island in the canine training circuit. However felt I had to be a 'responsible adult" and keep my focus on the big picture. I put an abundant amount of time into my status in the Utility Company & I felt I actually retire from that company one day.

In spite of all the encouragement from my family & friends, to work in the canine training circuit, I was resistant to committing myself to the idea of being in my own business. I kept thinking my life was "on course" and I just wasn't ready nor did I think I was cut out to be a professional canine trainer on a full time basis.

As I mentioned, the Utility Company was growing in leaps & bounds. However the company was having a difficult time keeping up with the new business demand. Sales Managers (including myself) were struggling to receive compensation for large sales. The larger our sales, the more involved the internal process. It seemed like an impossible feat. Large sales were not moving through the internal systems fast enough. It was taking months for new fiber networks to complete. It appeared as though the internal processes were not working efficiently. It was frustrating at best.

I recognized a major necessity in the company to coordination internal efforts & manage large projects. Large sales /projects required new fiber construction, network management, equipment ordering, installation and much more. All of which seemed to go into, the legendary corporate "black whole". It was taking so long to complete network builds that some of our new clients began cancelling their orders. The sales team couldn't get compensated for their efforts since the orders were not completing and therefore the company was losing an enormous amount of money in addition to losing their talented sales people.

After roughly a year of working in a sales capacity, I too became weary. As a single mother, it was difficult at best to wait to get completion dates, more importantly, wait to receive monetary compensation.

I wrote a "Business Plan" which would later be presented to the Senior Management Team. The business plan included a New Project Management Team that would oversee the internal processes and new construction projects. This would be the opportunity of a life time. Amazingly the Senior Management Team approved the business plan. A new chapter was unfolding in my life and I couldn't be happier about the new challenge.

I was provided the "means" to create a new division. The Project Management Team was born. This team would not only fix the internal issues that were broken, but also created new internal processes for the company that would address many of the issues we were facing. Within, 30 days, large sales began to complete in a more timely fashion. Cash flow was back.

The Project Management Division was my new baby. Now I was part of the Senior Management Team. My division, over the next several months, would make the company more productive, save the company hundreds of thousands of dollars, and finally the sales team was able to get compensated in a timely fashion. I hired and trained 18 employees. I was determined to make a difference and I clearly I was doing such.

A very clever person once told me...successful people do, what unsuccessful people refuse to do". As far as I understand it, the only place the word "**Work**" comes "after" the word "**Success**" is in the dictionary. I was pressing forward, working hard to make a name for myself. The Senior Management Team was impressed with my determination and I was on a mission to prove them right.

As I mentioned, the company was growing fast, essentially too fast! Data & Voice services was their startup division. Unfortunately the company felt they had ˝over hired ˝ employees in almost every division. "Corporate" decided major layoffs were in order. I was an integral part of choosing the employees who would stay with the company. Meeting after grueling meeting, it was heartbreaking & a very emotional time. After almost 10 years in the company, having survived through (4) four major lay-offs, I was now running a division that in essence, was running *me* into the ground. I was working 7 days a week & long hours to keep up with the business demand, and although I was still very successful, I was tired, weary and praying for a change in my life. I wanted and needed more flexibility to raise my son and enjoy life as it was meant to be.

## A Time of Change

**As the universe would have it, change was on the way**. While in my office one rainy Monday morning at 7:30 AM, word was buzzing around referencing yet another lay-off. I was confused, as I was part of the Senior Manager Team that would normally make those decisions. It was unusual, to say the least, that I would had no idea of what was about to happen. As mentioned, previous to this day, I was an essential part of the decision making team with the prior lay-offs. However not this time.

This particular lay off was different. **Surprisingly enough, I was to learn, my "Senior Management" position was eliminated from the company budget**. Furthermore, unbeknownst to me, I had being training a young collogue, straight out of college, for a few months prior. I later found out that he was actually being groomed, by me, to fill a *"similar"*, however, *"renamed position"* at less than half my salary. **It was ugly!** It took me collectively twenty years in the Telecom Industry along with, as one might say, " blood, sweat and many tears" to earn my "Senior Management Position" yet it was gone in what seemed like an instant.

**My world was about to change as I knew it**. I was insecure and worried that I would not be able to provide for my son & me. For months following the layoff, I scurried to interview in the Telecom market hoping to replace, my safety net and land another "White Collar" position. The market place was dry and I wasn't having much luck securing a reasonably paying position that could support me and my son. Interview after interview, I was told I was **overqualified**. I was nervous about my future and questioned what the future would hold for me.

## How "THE" dog trainer began

My dear friend, Ross Coleman, had been by my side through it all. He was and still is a brilliant & very inspired man. He came up with the idea that I should "dive – head first" into the canine training circuit, full time. He began discussing it with me on the very day I lost my position at the Utility Company. He was persistent and eventually Ross as well as others collogues, family, friends etc. were able to convince me to move forward with what I today consider to be "my true life's calling". I began a full time career as a **Professional Master Canine Trainer**. It was one of the biggest decisions of my life. As it turns out I truly feel "**THIS**" **is my purpose in life.** Once I took the leap of faith, my life changed as I knew it - - forever. A new chapter in my world quickly unfolded. **Today, by the Grace of God, I never look back.**

Now, years later, I am inspired to share my experience, strength and knowledge with "canine parents" everywhere, in the hopes that you will embrace a unique method of canine training and understanding of the canine mind. **This book is about the simple canine mind and canine training made enjoyable & easy. This is "THE ONE MINUTE DOG TRAINER"**

**"Donna & Rocky"**

# Mission Statement

THE ONE MINUTE DOG TRAINER was developed by Donna Marie Casey. This program was designed to reach your canine in a happy & respectful manner that "they" will easily understand & enjoy. Your canine will be inspired to learn. This new training technique will stimulate and motivate your canine through "Proper Positive Reinforcement Techniques". Your canine will learn quicker and more efficiently when using "Leading Edge Hand Commands" & they will want to keep coming back for the enjoyment of learning.

This new method of canine training is training made easy & it is more effective than any other canine training not only for you (the New Canine Parent) but for Your New Canine. This book provides an accurate understanding of canine behavior, which will assist you in inspiring your canine to want to learn without the stress of harsh corrections.

**"The program requires one simple thing, your <u>commitment</u> and <u>consistency</u> to your new addition. This is one of the easiest canine training programs in the training circuit today. My concept is simple, IT works - if <u>YOU</u> work it – ONE MINUTE at a time!**

At "THE" dog trainer LI, Inc. it is my mission to assist you in achieving the happiness you desired when you decided to add a new addition to your family. I believe that "coaching you" enabling you to understand & teach your canine, can be simple when you learn why canines do the things they do and how to address both new & old behaviors.

I will be provide you with the necessary tools to an enriched life with your new canine. The transition of bringing a new canine into your home can be a fairly easy one, when you establish healthy boundaries from the start. In this book I will help you address canine training using an accurate understanding of the canine mind, canine behavior and new, simple training techniques.

**THE ONE MINUTE DOG TRAINER** is a life changing program that will enable you to enjoy your new canine without the heartache of living through messy house breaking, teething, jumping, aggression and destructive adolescent canine behavior. This training program works and will simplify your life if you are consistent and committed to your new pet.

**Training 1 or many, THE ONE MINUTE DOG TRAINER**
**Was designed to make training easy & enjoyable!**

# Chapter 1

## New Canine - Welcome

If you are reading this book chances are you have decided to add a new addition to your life & family. So now what? Whether you have owned a canine before or perhaps this is your first time as a "canine parent", your life is about to change. Many people make a very common mistake. They instinctively compare their *new* puppy/dog to other puppies/dogs that they have owned in the past. However, every canine has their own personality. **No two canines are the same.** Even if they are littermates or perhaps come from the same blood lines, like humans, canines have their own personality's, likes and dislikes.

Young canines, for the most part, are simple minded. They follow their instinctual behaviors. When canines are born, they begin roaming in their whelping box with their mothers and siblings. They have no worries. Eating, playing, sleeping and even eliminating, "just happens". For the first 6 to 8 weeks, with very little human interaction, their life are very simple. Their vision quickly begins to develop and in a short period of time, they learn how to get around. Life is one big adventure, in their very "small" world. They are born into a simple life were sleeping, eating and even play is all done in one safe environment. All their needs are attended to. Sound familiar? Yes, the canine life can be compared, in many ways, to a "human infant".

Here is the exception, soon after birth approximately 6 to 8 weeks, once weaned from their mother's milk, canines are of age to be on 'their own". These young beings are separated from life as they know it. Off they go! Sent into a new environment, in essence a whole new world. Think about it! What a shock it must be to a young life! They no longer have the comfort and protection of their mother. They are not with their siblings, their needs are changing and now they are quickly becoming independent beings. Then, a new "human" comes into their life and life, as they know it, is about to change.

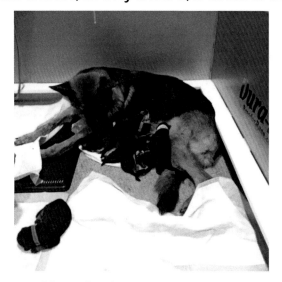

**"Wendy – A New Canine Mother & Her New Babies"**

## New Canine - Welcome

Life for a new canine life is perceived as one big adventure. Change can & usually is overwhelming. All at once we (humans) expect these young beings to sleep in a new place, more than likely – this new pup is alone, perhaps for the first time in their lives, they are expected to eat when <u>we</u> say so, play with new toys and eliminate exactly <u>when</u> & <u>where</u> <u>we</u> <u>want</u> them to "go"!

In this chapter you will discover helpful hints that will assist you when bringing a new canine into your home and connecting them with their new human family (pack). The following pointers should prove to make for an easy transition. If you have knowledge about your canine, you will have the power to make his/her transition an easy one.

**"I want them ALL! Sometimes choosing can be difficult"**

## *Bringing Your New Canine Home*

As humans, we are able to understand that moving from one home to another can be a difficult transition at best. Without a doubt, though we (humans) understand that our new home will ultimately be better than our old one, although we have this knowledge, change can still create anxiety and tension in our lives.  We are for, the most part, fairly organized. Still, packing up our lives then unpacking, arranging furniture,  etc. can be so stressful. We may find it difficult trying to sleep in a new place. Change, for most humans, is not easy.

Now try to imagine a similar transition for a young or older canine, who is unable to "reason" as human being can. They are removed from their homes – perhaps leaving a breeder or a, shelter etc.  No doubt moving can and usually is, very difficult & stressful for most canines. Below you will find a New Canine Checklist that will help facilitate a good start.

**"Moving can be difficult & very stressful for most canines"**

# New Canine Checklist

*What to bring when you pick up your pup.*

- **Collar or harness**
- **Leash** (Will assist with getting your pup to & from the car. Also needed to keep your new canine on the wee wee pad or in one section of your yard)
- **Travel crate** (For safe travel)
- **Paper towel** (For accidents that may occur on your car ride home)
- **Puppy Wipes** (To help clean your pup should an accident occur)

*What to have when you bring your puppy home.*

*For sleeping:*

- **Wire or Metal Crate with divider** (Size is important)
- **A NEW Towel for inside the crate** (Or a crate liner)

*For Puppy protection:*

- **Important phone numbers** (Ex: Nearby emergency 24 hr. vet)
- **Current Medical Records**
- **Nutra Drops** (Used for blood sugar stabilization, especially for very small canines such as tea cup breeds.)
- **Flea & Tick prevention** (Should be used 12 months a year)
- **Heart Worm protection** (Applicable when your pup weighs enough)
- **Hydrogen peroxide** (To induce vomiting if ever needed)
- **Liquid Benadryl** (Used for many allergies, anxiety & more)

*For Potty Training:*

- **Wee wee pads**
- **Wee wee pad holder** (to ensure your new canine does not chew the wee wee pads)
- **Poop bags** (For easy cleanup & outside training)
- **Special treats for potty**
- **Enzyme-based cleaner** (Be sure to use an **enzyme based cleanser** specifically made to eliminate the order and remove the enzymes of canine urination & defecation)
- **Potty bells for the door** (For outside transition or house breaking)

*For Canine safety:*

- Baby gates (Ensures your canine remains in one small section of the house at first)
- Deterrent - ex. Bitter Apple or Citronella Spray (Used to deter your new pup from chewing on furniture & in some cases mouthing on humans)

*For Meal Time:*

- Water & food bowls (Appropriately sized for your new canine)
- Food (Check the <u>Name Brand</u> of the <u>current food</u> your new pup is now eating with your breeder or wherever you are obtaining your pup. *You will want to keep your canine on the same food for a while to avoid intestinal issues*
- Vitamins (Assists in healthy digestion)
- Skin & Coat Conditioner (Helps create healthy hair follicles from the inside – out so your pup will shed less and have a healthy, shiny coat)
- Joint Mobility (Should be used to assist in solidifying joints for younger canines and/or will help older canine mobility)
- Food Storage Bin (Keeping your canine's food fresh is important and it will preserve the vitamin intake in your canine's food)

*For play time:*

- Chew toys/bones (Assists with teething for young pups and satisfies the need to gnaw for the older canines)
- Plush squeaker toys (Adds excitement to play)
- Rope toys (Good for flossing puppy teeth & helps the older canines with chewing)
- Fetch toys (Ex: Safe balls & flying discs)
- Puppy/Dog shampoo (e.g.: Oatmeal shampoo)
- Puppy/Dog conditioner (to keep his/her coat soft & manageable)

*For Grooming:*

- Brush/comb suited to your breed's coat type & size
- Ear cleaning solution
- Cotton balls
- Nail clippers
- Canine tooth brush
- Canine toothpaste

*First aid kit for CANINES:*

- Benadryl (Used for allergies, bug bite & more)
- Wound spray
- Gauze
- Self-clinging bandage
- Eye wash

# Chapter 2

## *Canine's Take Time to Adjust*

### Canines', old or young, need time to adjust to new changes in environment and daily routine.

- Take it slow – this transition can take a few weeks.
- Try not to over – compensate for any hard times you feel that your new addition may have experienced in the past by being too permissive.
- Don't feel that you need to constantly entertain your new canine. When you are constantly engaging with your new canine, you will be establishing a pattern you may not want to live with.
- Too much freedom can be unhealthy, eventually you will want/need to confine your new canine in order to potty train/house break train, however they will not respond kindly to being in a crate or a confined area if you are constantly holding and interacting with them. Inevitably they will cry, whine and bark when confined as they will feel insecure without you. You want your new pup to feel content in his/her new living environment.

**"Max & Leo - Eventually grew out of their shared crate"**

**This is their new Crate – Custom Designed to keep them together**

## *Introducing Your New Addition to Your Home*

- Whether young or old, moving a canine from one place to another into a different environment with a new "human family" is stimulating enough for the time being.
- Try to **limit** the amount of **company** you have for the **first few weeks,** to make the process less stressful.
- Give your new canine time to adjust. Like any new relationship, this one also requires <u>time</u>, <u>patience</u> and <u>understanding</u>. Each canine warms up at their own pace, which may differ from your previous experiences with other canines.

## *Change can take a Few Weeks*

Change in environment for a canine, young or old, can trigger temporary behavioral problems.

- For example, depending on his/her age some canines will urinate in unexpected places, while others might to want to chew things.
- Some may feel overwhelmed at first and want to hide or run away while others take a more defensive position.
- As "pack animals," canines will test you to find out where they stand in the social hierarchy of your family.  You & your family are now, their "new human pack."
- Living in a crate provides little stimulation. In a new environment, a canine may become over-stimulated and become "testy "or hyperactive. Be patient!

## *Change can take a Few Weeks*

- As soon as you arrive home, show your new addition where his/her toilet area (potty spot) is located. This might be a wee wee pad or designated place on your property, depending on the breed type and age of your canine.
- Show your new addition where the crate/bed, food and water dishes are located.
- While <u>supervised,</u> give your new addition "a little" freedom and space to explore new surroundings.
- It's best to plan ahead, so your home is puppy/dog proof and free of any potential hazards.

## "Look what I found?"

- Chewing on wood can be dangerous, wood can splinter & may cause some serious internal damages. Therefore the new roaming area should be puppy/dog proof <u>before</u> allowing your new canine to roam around. Understand that even while under supervision, it only takes a moment for something unintentional to become a major event.

*Provide your new canine with his own living area, a safe haven where he/she can go to be alone.*

- Your canine's living area should <u>NOT</u> be an <u>isolated</u> area such as in a basement, or behind closed doors. Canines need to feel part of their new pack. They will want to see you, be close to you or be able to hear you, which provides them with comfort. Some canines may be frighten of a crate. Do not force your canine into the crate especially when introducing the crate for the first time. Do not close the crate door and walk away.

**"Let them get comfortable inside the crate <u>before</u> you close the crate door"**

## Introducing Your Canine to the Crate for the First Time

- Bring a few *crate safe toys* with you when introducing the crate for the first time.
- Leave the crate door open, let your canine smell around the crate.
- The idea is to create an atmosphere that your canine will want to be a part **of**.
- Squeak a new toy in front of the crate door, place the squeaker toy at the entrance of the crate and watch your canine's reaction. Let him/her enter then, immediately exit if they choose.
- Allow your canine to enter and exit the crate <u>several times</u> on their own.
- <u>Stay with them</u> as they explore.
- If the crate is large enough, you may want to positon yourself somewhat inside the crate to let him/her know it is safe.
- Your canine will need to feel secure <u>before </u>you close the crate door.

More on assisting your canine becoming comfortable with their crate later on in this chapter.

# "Be inventive! Make it Fun!"

## New Canine Living Area

- Be careful around doors to prevent escape. Since your canine's surroundings are new, his/her instinct may be to run the moment a door is open. This is not because they do not want to be with you, but for reasons such as, they think they can find familiar surroundings if they run or they may simply want to run for freedom.
- <u>Keep a leash or a tether</u> (a light cotton rope) on your new dog or puppy when you are home. This will provide you with <u>control</u> without having to grab or startle him/her.
- Soak the leash/tether in a deterrent or mouthwash <u>first</u>, this might deter your pup from chewing on it.

**"Keep your new canine on a <u>tether</u> or <u>lead</u> will help you keeep them safe"**

- Canines are pack animals and live by a social hierarchy so <u>establishing consistent rules from the beginning </u>is extremely important. For example:  Discuss with your family whether or not your new canine should be permitted on your furniture.  If <u>you</u> are <u>not allowing</u> your canine <u>on the furniture</u> however, <u>your</u> <u>children</u> are <u>encouraging</u> him/her to join them on the furniture, your family is sending <u>mixed messages </u>to your canine.

- Be sure to <u>discuss the rules</u> in advance with your family. This will elevate confusion for both your family but more importantly, your new canine. Your entire household should be consistent & be in agreement with the house rules. Establish some simple "wanted behaviors" <u>before</u> your new pup arrives. Write the rules down so everyone in your household is clear about them. By doing this you will prevent your canine from thinking he/she is in the driver's seat!

**This is "Sunday" and she enjoys being a Sunday driver."**

- Establish schedule for playtime. Puppies & dogs enjoy play. Most canine's want to engage with you. At first, some may be shy, hesitant or frighten. Don't force play, be casual about it. Try not to overwhelm your new canine with tons of new toys all at one time.

**"Canine's love to play"**

- Place a few toys on the floor and watch which of the toys peaks his/her interest. He/she will show you the ones that stimulate them. At that point, you can <u>gradually</u> attempt to interact with him/her. This way your new pup will not be overwhelmed by "you" as well as all the new toys.

**"Gizmo is very content without his toys for the moment"**

- In general, canines love to be outside, especially in nice weather. For the younger ones, be sure <u>not</u> to take them too far without them having had <u>all of their medical shots</u>. Remember their bodies are no longer using their mother's immune system. They can pick up harmful disease very quickly. If your young pups is small, just holding them while walking around outside can be an enjoyable experience for both of you. It's the fresh air you are wanting to expose them to, most times you will find your canine will sleep like a baby after being exposed to the fresh air.

**Sleeping like a baby"**     **"Close supervision is required"**

- If you home has a deck or a driveway *(that has been previously canine proofed)* you may let your pup momentarily outside to feel the ground and smell around for a bit. It's all new to them, so do not over stimulate them by allowing them to stay outside too long. Short visits outside can be healthy. Just like a human infant, fresh air will help them to relax.

- Older canines may be taken for walks off your property **as long as** they are not sick. It will diversify their environment and allow for early socialization. Of course check with your veterinarian **prior** to engaging in walks off your property. It's better to be safe than sorry.

**"LEXI"**

**"GIZMO"**

**"Be sure your canine's has medical clearence _before_ socializing "**

# Chapter 3

## *Crate Training*

## Why Crate Training can be Successful

It I my professional opinion that crate training can be extremely effective and successful when done correctly. Realizing in the wild, a canine mother would create a small environment to protect her young from danger. This is referred to as a den. She creates the den to keep her pups warm, dry and to feed them safely. Eventually she teaches her pups to eliminate outside the den.

**"Canine mothers keep their young safe in a small environment known as a den"**

The theory is - when young canines <u>eat</u> and <u>sleep</u> in "their" secure environment, (crate) they will typically <u>not</u> want to eliminate there. After some time, when your canine is no longer having "elimination" mistakes in his/her crate, you can feed him/her outside the crate. Crating creates a safe place where young/new canines can sleep & eat while feeling secure. This is the reason I, along with many other professional canine trainers, suggest crate training.

Depending upon the age and breed of your pup, you should begin with <u>short periods of crating</u> and work your way to longer stretches of time. The correct timelines will be discussed in further detail a bit later. It is important that you <u>start immediately</u> (as soon as new pup arrives). Too much freedom, from the start can, and usually "will" hinder crate training success.

As "human parents" we show much concern for the safety of our infants and toddlers. We never leave an infant or toddler unattended unless they are secured. We stay close, much of the time, listening to a baby monitor & walking in and out of their rooms. Then once our young ones begin to fuss, we go running to pick up our bundle of joy, knowing that when they must be fussing for a reason. Usually a diaper change or it might be feeding time.

For most of our infant and toddler's young life, they are under close watch. We place our young ones in a playpen, crib, bassinet, car seat etc. (*confinement*) to keep him/her safe when we cannot physically be with them. We consistently keep a close watch on our young humans so we can attend to their every need.

The same is true with young canines. The younger the canine, the more supervision is required. They are just like infants/toddlers only, unfortunately, without diapers. Because they are young and curious, left unattended they will undoubtedly get into trouble and for sure they will eliminate whenever they feel the need.

## "Look familiar? There are definite similarities."

Many new "canine parents" feel bad leaving their young canines in a crate. It is "thought" to be "cruel". However the truth is, we do the exact same thing (confinement) with our young human infants & toddlers. There are many similarities between human infants/toddlers and young canines. Both of them require an enormous amount of sleep. When they awaken is it usually due to a "need". For example, they need to, or already have, eliminated or perhaps they are hungry. Of course both human infants and young canines require human interaction, play time etc. After eating, eliminating & having human interaction, human infants and canines typically become whiney & ornery since they are tired as their little bodies are growing so fast & therefore require an enormous amount of sleep.

## Crate Training – Why Confinement?

Canines need down time and a lot of sleep. Young canines, while sleeping are experiencing accelerated growth. The same amount of growth a <u>human</u> experiences in approximately <u>18 years,</u> is happening to a <u>young</u> <u>canine</u> within <u>12 to 15 months</u>. Hence is why house breaking (potty training) does not take as much time with most canines as it does with young humans. The canine's muscles grow at an execrated rate making it possible to "hold" in a short period of time. Usually by 6 months of age, a canine is able to "hold" in the crate, if confined properly, 4 to 6 hours during the day.

Look at the vast amount of growth that has taken place with this canine "Capone" in a little over a year. The growth is enormous. Even though smaller canines may not "appear" to have the same amount of dramatic growth, their rate of growth is similar, just to a smaller degree.

## Over Stimulation

When young canines are overstimulated, they become feistier, especially when teething. Overstimulation of young canines can cause additional unwanted behaviors such as mouthing, biting, & jumping. Most of these behaviors increase with overstimulation primarily because the canine is physically uncomfortable due to teething & accelerated growth. Constant over excitement and interaction with humans creates a great deal of canine body movement. Movement will make your canine need to eliminate more often. Therefore they will have frequent accidents, especially if left unattended.

# 10 Important Reasons to Properly Confine Your Canine

1. Confining your canine provides a <u>safe environment</u> for your canine. Since the day they were born, they were in a confined either in a corral or play pen then eventually into a crate. If you start early enough, you should not have any negative reaction to confinement.
2. Your canine will quickly become acclimated to <u>your schedule</u>, instead of you working vigorously around theirs.
3. Confining your canine sets <u>healthy boundaries.</u>
4. When your canine is confined (to a small area) his/her <u>energy will usually remain calm</u>. Allowing him/her the proper sleep they need to grow and mature.
5. Confining your canine allows <u>you</u> to <u>provide</u> <u>structure required</u> to properly house train & potty training.
6. Since most canines do not like to eliminate where they sleep and/or eat, "<u>you</u>" are teaching them to <u>alert you</u> when they have to do their business. As he/she will usually bark or whine when they need to eliminate.

"HE LOOKS VERY COMFORTABLE"

7. If you are confining your canine properly, it will make house breaking successful in a very short period of time, reducing many unwanted accidents.
8. Confinement will allow you to be able to take your canine anywhere without worry or fear of your canine will have unwanted accidents in public places & other people's homes.
9. You will <u>not</u> become a human "doggie door", needing to be <u>accessible</u> to your canine 24 hours a day.
10. Confining your canine will <u>protect your home</u> from <u>unwanted destructive behavior.</u>

## *Avoiding Destructive Behavior*

This below was a client's living room, after having left their 8 month old Rottweiler out of her crate for a short time, unattended. They owners truly believed she would be "safe" for a short period time, since she was so "well behaved" under their supervision.

## **Destructive Behavior**

"Young & sometimes older canines become bored quickly. This can lead to not only unwanted destructive behavior, but also harmful & sometimes <u>deadly physical results</u>."

# Crate Training

## Crate Size <u>DEFINATELY</u> Matter

<u>Choosing the right size is crucial!</u> When buying a new crate for your canine, be sure to purchase a crate that addresses his/hers potential growth and make sure it comes with a divider so you can adjust the size as your canine grows.

**"Make sure the crate has a <u>divider</u>"**

      The following information focuses on the 'big picture' and is a 'step-by-step' guide to assist you in giving your canine the help he/she will need from the beginning. It will also help you to avoid the most common pitfalls with house-training (wee wee pad training) and provide you with the answers to the questions you may have if you have never crate trained a canine in the past.

## Start Upon Arrival

It's important to get your canine's housebreaking started right away – literally on the first day that you bring your canine home. Canines mentally absorb absolutely everything around them. They learn amazingly quickly. Which is great when they're learning the things you're wanting to teach them- not so great when they're picking up bad habits or figuring out how to do things that you don't want them to do!

Canines are creatures of habit, they learn through repetition. Once a canine has done something 3 or 4 times, it can now be a habit. After a short while it will becomes "instinctive behavior" that you may not want.

Hence is why it's crucial to make sure your new pup doesn't have the opportunity to make too many potty-training mistakes. A few 'mistakes' are inevitable during this phase, but regular 'accidents' will quickly become a habit and that's when real problems begin.

## Give Your Canine a Potty Break - FIRST

Make sure your pup has been outside or to the wee wee pad to 'do his/her business' before you place him/her in the crate, even for a short period of time.

This way when he/she begins fussing in the crate right away, you know for sure, he/she doesn't have an urgent need to 'go'. This will cut down on the chances of elimination in the crate.

## Give His/her 1 or 2 Favorite Toys

It's a good idea to have a special, safe toy or bone (or two) for your pup to play with when they are in their crate. This will eliminate possible boredom and help him/her to forget he's not outside the crate running around.

"Make sure the toys you choose for his/her crate are crate safe."

## Stay Close

**Stay close by at first.** Young canine & many older rescues may feel happier and usually feel reassured if they can ˝smell' you near them. They want to be with ˝their humans˝ and if you disappear from sight the first time he/she is placed in their crate, your little guy could become frighten. If you have to leave the room, calmly calling out to him/her (randomly) can be helpful for them to hear your voice so that they know you haven't deserted them.

## Ignore the Fussing!

When you first begin crate training young canines, it is rarely going to be *all* smooth sailing. Almost all puppies will fuss and cry the first few times they are placed in their crate. Remember, they are alone perhaps for the first time so they will want to be near you!

**If you take your pup out of the crate as soon he/she begins whining I can almost guarantee they will whine even louder and longer the next time.**

## Spending Time in the Crate (**Start with short periods of time in the crate.**)

Placing a young canines crate beside your bed or in your bedroom at night will allow you to hear them. They need to be somewhere you can hear him (although you may wish you couldn't hear them at 2am). Remember, they are young and will need to 'eliminate' at <u>least once during the night.</u>

Crate training young canines during the night time is easier if you make sure your little one has had a potty break and <u>hasn't had access to drinking water</u> after <u>approximately 7pm - 8pm.</u> Like human infants, canines can most likely sleep for several hours before needing to do their ˝business˝ again.

<u>Do</u> <u>not</u> <u>ignore</u> little ones & young ones crying in the <u>middle of the night,</u> as it is very possible, he/she may <u>not</u> **be able to hold** when they are too small or very young. Ignoring them will force them to do their ˝business ˝in the crate. This will make housebreaking much more difficult.

This stage only lasts a <u>short while</u> and you'll be glad you made the decision to crate train your canine.

# Hourly Crate Intervals - by Age of Your Canine

The following guideline will assist you in getting a solid start with house breaking. Depending on size and breed and how much food or water your young canine consumes, these hourly intervals may vary to some degree.

One thing to keep in mind is that even with the following a schedule, young canines should be taken to the elimination spot as soon as they wake up, after eating or drinking, and after actively playing.

## 6-12 WEEKS

Daytime: Every hour to hour and a half.
Night time: 3-4 hours should be sufficient, assuming they haven't eaten or drank less than three hours before bedtime.

## 12-16 WEEKS

Daytime: Hours increase to about every 2 hours
Nighttime: Hours increase to 4-6 hours

## 4-5 MONTHS

Daytime: Every 3 hours
Nighttime: Roughly 6 hours

## 6-7 MONTHS

Daytime: Hours increase to 4 hours
Nighttime: Remains around 6 hours.

## 8-11 MONTHS

Daytime: Hours vary between 5-6 hours
Nighttime: Roughly 8 hours.

## 12 MONTHS AND OLDER

Daytime: Your pup can hold for **up to 8 hours**
Nighttime: Anywhere from 8-10 hours. This estimate may differ with older canines depending on how well their bladders are since they've aged or if there are any health problems that could affect their schedules.

## Don't Use the Crate for Punishment

Your canine's crate is supposed to be a safe and happy place. It is the location he/she sleeps and eats. It is where he goes when you're not home. It is his/her sanctuary. If you use this sanctuary for punishment, it will lose its intended value. It will no longer serve as a safe haven. Being confined for punishment in his/her crate can breed resentment and unwanted destructive behaviors when they are released from the crate.

## Crate & Separation Anxiety

Make the crate a positive experience. Most young canines or older rescues are kept in a play pen or a den with other pups. Now they are alone. So the first few times you crate your canine they will undoubtedly create a noisy ruckus. They'll cry, bark, whine and let you know they are miserable. They might feel frightened. Investigate some fairly new items on the market today for example a heartbeat pillow or puppy. This may provide the comfort your canine needs to overcome his/her fear of being alone.

Have faith & patience, crate training your canine can be the right decision. Your canine, in very short time, will become comfortable with their crate if <u>you</u> don't give up.

## Covering the Crate May Help

Like a bird being covered in their cage, covering the crate may calm your canine down. When the crate is covered, they may feel more secure. When they can see you they <u>will</u> want to be with you.

**"You can find crate covers readily available on the internet"**

28

## Cleaning up the accidents

In the beginning your Canine will inevitably have accidents, expect it and be prepared! Get rid of the scent immediately. Use an <u>enzyme based product,</u> specifically made to clean up canine elimination. Take a look at the examples below. Using other *"scented household products"* can and usually does disrupt potty training as the scent of urine or defecation can still be present when not cleaned properly.

**"Easy clean up products, <u>specifically</u> <u>made</u> to <u>remove</u> <u>orders</u> from pet elimination."**

## State "<u>THE PLACE</u>"

Many new "canine parents" do not realize that it is <u>YOU</u> who is teaching your canine the rules. <u>EVERY TIME</u> you take your canine to the <u>elimination spot YOU</u> must say <u>where/what</u> the spot is called. For example: Using your canine's name & having him/her <u>on the lead</u>, bring him/her to the wee wee pad. As your pup is <u>standing on the wee wee pad,</u> say something like: Lily "POTTY HERE" – <u>while you are pointing to the wee wee pad.</u> Continue to repeat as needed. Once your pup has actually done his/her business ON THE PAD...Praise and reward <u>ON THE PAD</u>, stating "YES! Good Potty <u>HERE</u>!" as you are pointing <u>at the wee wee pad.</u>

However if you are house breaking your canine <u>EVERY TIME</u> you are ready to open the door & take your canine to eliminate "outside", As you are opening the door, use your <u>canine's name</u> & <u>the same words</u>. Say something to the effect of: Rover, "POTTY OUTSIDE?" Repeat the words every time you open the door to take your canine outside to relieve themselves. Once your pup has actually completed his/her business <u>OUTSIDE, praise and reward</u> <u>OUTSIDE</u>. Praise them -"YES! Good Potty <u>OUTSIDE</u>!" as you are pointing to the ground, as you are still standing OUTSIDE.

## "Yes! Good Potty <u>OUTSIDE</u> guys!"

Your canine needs to understand <u>THE PLACE</u> "you want them to eliminate. It is not a canine instinct to read the human mind. It's only logical that your canine would become confused if "<u>YOU" are NOT repeatedly stating the rules.</u> Canines learn by repetition.

## *Why do some canines hide to do "their business"?*

Since the day your canine was born, whenever they needed to "to do their business" they simply stopped, <u>where ever they were standing</u> and do their business. Now they are living in a human household. Your canine does not instinctually understand that you are changing the rules. Most "canine parents "the moment you catch your pup eliminating on the floor or the carpet, instinctively <u>YELL</u> the word "NOOOOOOOOOOOOO!!!"

At this point your canine thinks you *are* <u>correcting the URINATION or DEFECATION.</u> They <u>DO NOT</u> understand you are actually correcting the <u>PLACE.</u>

Instead of using the word "<u>NO</u>" I recommend that you <u>interrupt your canine's behavior</u> by <u>making a loud noise</u> with your mouth such as– <u>HEY</u>! Or clapping your hands loudly while on your way to pick <u>your canine up during the "act".</u> Most canines will stop eliminating when they hear a loud noise directed at them or when being picked up because they are startled. <u>QUICKLY</u> get him/her to the elimination spot to finish their business.

30

## *Rewarding the Behavior & the Correct Place*

Since you are wanting your canine to understand that he/she is eliminating WHERE you want him/her to "go" (THE CORRECT PLACE), get happy WHEN & WHERE "the deed" is COMPLETED. Utilize a special treat that is only used for potty. Use a treat with a good strong scent. A small morsel goes a long way. They will be eliminating a lot in the beginning so do not over reward them. You will need to be patient and wait until they have completed the task. A COMMON CANINE PARENTS MISTAKE IS TO BEGIN TO PRAISE YOUR CANINE BEFORE THEY HAVE COMPLETEDE THEIR BUSINESS. This can be distracting your canine. Using your words too soon & treating before the "deed" is complete will stop your canine from eliminating. If you release a treat to your canine before they have finished elevating themselves, your canine will stop eliminating (due to your distraction) then begin eliminating again, because you rewarded too soon.

IMPORTANT: Rewarding or praising your canine on the kitchen floor, "AWAY" from the wee wee pad or rewarding "INSIDE" for eliminating "OUTSIDE" definitely will send your canine a mixed message. They are simple mined beings who are just beginning to learn "YOUR" new rules. Your canine will think you are rewarding their "elimination", MEANWHILE you are wanting to "REWARD" the elimination "PLACE". This will cause a lot of confusion to your young canine and unnecessary accidents.

## *Rewarding the Behavior & the Place*

Reward ON the wee wee pad!

**Good Potty Right Here!**

# Potty Bells – Signaling the Need to Eliminate "Outside"

Most young canines are <u>unaware</u> they need to <u>give you a signal</u> that they need to eliminate, no less outside.  If your canine is not providing you with a signal, he/she will need a way of telling you he/she needs to go "outside". Some canines put their head down & begin to circle however if you aren't nearby to see the signs, they will just do their business right where they are.  In such cases, using <u>a potty bell</u> on or near the exit door that you are using when taking your canine to do their business can be helpful.

<u>Every time</u> you bring your canine to the exit door, <u>YOU</u> must <u>tap the bells</u> with your hand and <u>say the same words</u>. Example "Potty Outside" After tapping the bell a few times, <u>without showing</u> your canine, <u>place a touch of peanut butter or yogurt on the lowest bell,</u> just before you think he/she may have to go do their business.  Walk your canine to the bells and let his/her "nose go to work".  Once he/she licks the substance off the bells GET Excited!!  Repeat the words "YES! Potty outside!"

**"The bell rings, your canine eliminates "outside"**

Each time your canine taps the bells with their nose, repeat the words you have been using when you were tapping the bells for them. "Yes! Potty outside". Do not repeat peanut butter trick too often or your canine will start going to the bells just for the peanut butter & he/she will not learn why the bells are there. <u>Repeat the same words, every time you take your canine to the exit door and show them you are pleased!</u> In no time, your canine will be heading to the door and hitting his/her nose on the potty bells to give you a signal he/she needs to do their business.

Potty training and/or house training <u>does not</u> have to be an impossible quandary. It can instead be viewed as your first chance to build a bond with your canine by teaching your canine the rules.  <u>You</u> must begin to understand his/her needs & be patient. By using praise and using the correct (same) "simple 1 or 2 words, every time your canine achieves and completes eliminating, you are teaching him/her "<u>what to do</u>", more importantly, "<u>WHERE</u>" to do it!!!

## Crate Training Guidelines

      Crate Training, House Breaking, Potty Training is <u>your responsibility.</u>  How quickly your canine achieves the task depends on <u>how consistent you are</u> with him/her.  What works for one canine does not necessarily work for all.  Be creative, like human toddler's, they are beginning to learn about you & you are beginning to learn about them.  Sometimes ... it just takes time.

**"Much like human toddlers - they are just learning"**

*Outside Transition*

**House Breaking - Outside Transition**

1. One of the first things you can do to assist your canine to eliminate outside is to allow your canine to use the wee wee pad in the house. When he/she needs to eliminate again, bring the newly used pad with fresh urine and/or deification to the elimination spot outside. Turn the used pad upside down and rub the fresh elimination on the grass. This is called "marking" for your canine. You are "marking the area" ("outside") with his/her own fresh scent. Most canines will want to "mark" over their scent. Make sure YOU take your canine on the leash to that specific elimination place. Allow your canine to smell & circle around in the area. Do not give them too much space, the more area they have to smell around, the more distracted they might become. After you have said "POTTY OUTSIDE" a few times, try not to look, talk or touch your canine as this might interrupt them. Allow him/her to explore the scent. Keep him/her in close range to the elimination spot you have marked for them. Have a potty treat ready. Using word "OUTSIDE" is the key. Then praising using the word "outside" - - "YES! Good Potty "OUTSIDE!"

2. If you have been using a wee wee inside for several weeks (until your canine has received all of their proper shots), some canines may be confused as to "what you want them to do (eliminate) when they go "outside". Brining the wee wee outside may be very helpful. Since they are unsure of eliminating anywhere other than inside, on a wee wee pad, bringing the wee wee pad outside may elevate some of the confusion. Bring a newly used pad outside and secure the corners of the pad with rocks or some sort of weight so it doesn't blow away. Take your canine to the secured pad, encourage your canine by using the same words "POTTY HERE", when he/she eliminates on the pad outside remember to praise. "YES! Good Potty "OUTSIDE!"

3. Using the same words AND adding the word OUTSIDE! When praising your canine say something similar for example: YES! Good Potty OUTSIDE!"

4. There are many products on the market today that can assist you in transitioning your canine to eliminate outside. Research the internet for these helpful devices. Take a look at the following.

By placing the smelly gadgets OUTSIDE, place them in the area you want your canine to eliminate, you are "marking" the desired elimination area for him/her. It's important to keep your canine on a leash, close to the elimination spot and stay with them until the deed is done. You will also find it helpful to place a piece of their own deification in the elimination areal. They will use their nose to figure it out. It may take some time for their little brains to "get it", but worry not, they all do!

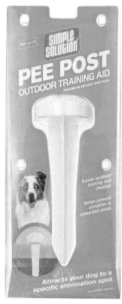 

**"Make it easy for them! - - Mark the teritory for them!"**

If you have been outside with your pup for more than 20 minutes, bring your canine inside and place them back in the crate to 10 or 15 minutes. When they start to fuss, bring them directly outside again to the elimination spot. Repeat taking your canine outside, then back to the crate, if he/she does not eliminated, until your canine eliminates outside.

Be sure to praise the PLACE as well as the DEED!

*Controlling Your Canine's <u>Input</u> Will Help You Control the <u>Output</u>*

*"Recommended" <u>Water intake</u>: Per day, by canine weight.*

| **<u>Weight</u>** | **<u>8 oz. glasses of water</u>** |
|---|---|
| Up to 10 lbs. | 1 ¼ glasses |
| Up to 20 lbs. | 2 ½ glasses |
| Up to 40 lbs. | 5 glasses |
| Up to 80 lbs. | 10 glasses |

*"Recommended" <u>Food intake</u>: Per day, by canine weight.*

| **<u>Canine Weight</u>** | **<u>Amount of daily food intake</u>** |
|---|---|
| Up to 15 lbs. | ½ - 1 cup |
| 16 to 25 lbs. | 1 – 1 ½ cups |
| 26 to 40 lbs. | 1 ½ - 2 ½ cups |
| 41 to 60 lbs. | 2 ½ - 3 ½ cups |
| 61 to 80 lbs. | 3 ½ - 4 ½ cups |
| 81 to 100 lbs. | 4 ½ - 6 cups |
| Over 100 lbs. | 6 cups + ½ cup for each add'l 20 lbs. |

Note: (1) cup equates to an 8 oz. cup. It is always best to consult with your veterinarian, especially if your canine is under 10 pounds or is on medication which may require additional water and/or food intake.

## Controlling Your Canine's Input

Most new "canine parents" feel it is necessary to leave an unlimited water supply their new pets.  Unless your canine is under 5 lbs. OR you are directed by your veterinarian for a medical reasons to allow your pup access to water, allowing your canine to graze water, when they choose, will make potty training / housebreaking more difficult. If your canine is consistently drinking small amounts of water, they will have to eliminate more often.  Making it almost impossible for you to know <u>when</u> they need to "eliminate".

I highly recommend that you <u>DO NOT</u> leave the water bowl <u>on the floor</u>. You can provide you canine water when warranted, usually 5 – 6 times a day, *including meal times*.  Once your pup is no longer drinking, by <u>removing the water bowl from the floor</u>, because the <u>bowl is not present</u> *(unseen)* your pup will be unsure when he/she will have access to water again.  Therefore when the water bowl is placed on the floor again, he/she will instinctually drink more water (at one time). Hence needing to relieve themselves more at one time.

The same is true with food.  I recommend <u>removing the food bowl</u> from the floor within <u>15 to 20 minutes</u> *if your canine is walking away from or has finished their meal.* If they are still eating (not grazing) leave the food bowl down for a few more minutes.  When you remove the food bowl, should there be food left, be sure to add the balance of the previous meal to their next meal.  It is NOT recommended that you <u>compromise</u> the <u>food intake</u> (amount) for your canine's weight & size. Your canine should be hungry by time the next feeding.

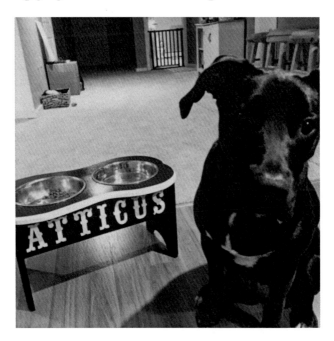

**"Food & Water Bowls should be suitable for the breed & size of your canine"**

When the food & water bowls are removed from the floor, your pup will most likely finish their next meal when fed. This is because they will be unsure when they will have access to food & water again. This makes it easier to gauge when your canine needs to eliminate, depending on the size of your canine. Usually young canines will need to eliminate within 5 to 15 minutes after eating. The smaller the canine the quicker they will need to eliminate.

Directly after eating and drinking your canine should be <u>confined</u> (crated) until they fuss, giving you a signal they need to eliminate. Usually canines will cry or bark, if not, watch your pup's body language. When your canine begins smelling around, placing their nose to the ground, beginning to circle their body, it usually means they need to eliminate. Quickly get the leash and take him/her to the elimination spot (wee wee pad or outside). Because you want your canine to get on "your" schedule, you will need to <u>make a schedule</u> for him/her. Take a look at the following feeding schedule. You can move the timeslots by an hour or two, up or down, <u>to suite your personal schedule</u>.

*New Puppy Daily Feeding Schedule*

New Puppy Daily Feeding Schedule: This schedule applies when your canine is <u>8 to 12 weeks</u> or if you are <u>feeding 3 times a day.</u>

# AM Schedule

### 7:00 am – 8:00 am

- <u>7:00 am</u> Wake up - Potty Time – Immediately take your canine from crate to potty spot
- Be sure to say "Potty <u>Here</u>" pointing to the wee wee pad or "Potty <u>Outside</u>"
- When your pup eliminates say: Good Potty <u>"HERE"</u> pointing to the wee wee pad or Good Potty <u>"OUTSIDE"</u> Reward <u>ON</u> the wee wee pad so they know <u>WHERE</u> you want them to eliminate or reward <u>outside</u>
- <u>7:15 am to 7:30 am</u> Play time – bonding time
- <u>7:30 am</u> Breakfast (leave food & water down for <u>20 to 30</u> minutes)
- Remove the food and water after 15-20minutes (DO NOT leave bowls down)
- <u>7:45 am</u> Potty Time
- No Elimination – *Keep your pup on a leash or inside the crate*
- Wait 5 to 10 minutes then take pup back to potty spot
- Be sure to say Potty <u>"Here"</u> or Potty <u>"Outside"</u>
- When your pup eliminated say  Good Potty <u>"HERE"</u> or Good potty <u>"OUTSIDE"</u>
- <u>Reward ON</u> the wee wee pad or outside


### 8:00 am – 10:00 am

- <u>8:00  am to 10:00 am</u> = Play time (Freedom only if your pup "eliminated")
- Once your pup has eliminated – free play time
- <u>10:00 am</u> Potty Time before Nap

### 10:00 am to 12:00

- <u>10:00 am to 12:00 pm</u> Nap time (back into the crate)

# Afternoon Schedule

### 12:00 pm – 1:00 pm

- 12:00 pm Potty Time – Immediately take your canine from crate to potty spot
- Be sure to say "Potty Here" pointing to the wee wee pad or "Potty Outside"
- No Elimination – Keep your pup on a leash or inside the crate
- Wait 5 to 10 minutes then take pup back to potty spot
- If your pup eliminated say  good potty "HERE" pointing to the wee wee pad or Good Potty "OUTSIDE"
- Reward ON the wee wee pad or outside
- 12:15 pm Lunch ( leave food & water down for 15 to 20 minutes)
- 12:30 pm Potty Time
- Be sure to say "Potty Here" or "Potty Outside"
- Light play – Do not over stimulate as your pup will be napping soon.
- 1:00 pm Potty Time before 2nd nap

### 1:00 pm – 5:00pm

- 1:00 pm to 5:00 pm Second Nap Time
- 5:00 Potty Time
- 5:30 pm – 6:00 pm Free play

## REMINDER: Reward the **PLACE NOT,** not just the **ACT**!

Remember you want to reward your canine for eliminating AT THE PLACE (the elimination spot).  If you reward him/her when they are standing on the kitchen floor away from the wee wee pad or you reward them when they are inside for eliminating outside you are sending your canine a mixed message.  They will think you are rewarding "elimination", they will NOT understand that you are rewarding the elimination spot.

# Evening Schedule

### 6:00 pm – 7:00 pm

- 6:00 pm Dinner Time (only leave food & water down for 15 to 20 minutes)
- Pick up food (DO NOT leave bowls down)
- 6:30 pm 15 – 20 minutes after food & water are taken up = Potty time
- 6:45 pm  Potty Time
- No Elimination – Keep your pup on a leash or back inside the crate
- Wait 5 to 10 minutes then take pup back to potty spot
- Once your pup has eliminated – free play time
- Be sure to say "Potty Here" pointing to the wee wee pad or  Potty "Outside"
- If your pup eliminated say  Good Potty HERE" or
  Good Potty OUTSIDE"
- Reward ON the wee wee pad or outside

### 7:00 pm – 10:45 pm

- 7:00 pm Play time (a small amount of water may be given)
- 9:00 pm Potty Time
- 9:15 pm Quiet Play time (try not to over stimulate your pup)
- 10:45 pm Potty time

### 11:00 pm
- Bedtime

Note:  Very young canines may not be able to hold for the entire night, especially if they have had access to water after 7:00pm.  If your canine is fussing at 2:00am, it most likely they need to eliminate.  Do not ignore a fuss in the middle of the night or you may waken to a messy crate. This could become a habit very quickly.

# Chapter 4

## Typical Canine Behavior

## *Digging*

Canines really like to dig. Most canines dig when it is warm outside so they can lay in the cool dirt. You'll have to train your canine to get him to stop. <u>When you catch him/her</u> in the act the command is "<u>Leave It!</u>" Commands will be discussed in further detail later on. <u>Immediately distract</u> him/her with a toy. It won't help to scold him/her after the digging is a done the deed. You need to <u>be consistent</u> and <u>correct your canine</u> <u>WHEN</u> he/she <u>is actually digging, not after the fact.</u>

Tip: Sometimes providing your canine with sandbox where he/she can go to town and dig all they want will prove helpful. Since sand has a different consistency than dirt, canines can learn the difference in texture. Take your canine to the sandbox and encourage them to dig there. They will feel the difference in the texture and along with your praise eventually they will learn **they can dig in the dig spot**. It takes time but has been known to be very effective. The key is <u>**YOU**</u> need to <u>stay with them</u> until they get it.

Some canines just want to instinctively burry a favorite toy or bone because it is fun finding it and digging it out. **Bring that special toy/bone to the sand box & pile on the praise when he/she begins to bury it.** This will help your canine learn that they can dig all day in the "dig spot".

"Bailey loves to dig"

"Using a Sand Box can help eliminate digging"

43

# Typical Canine Behavior

## Chewing

Canines, especially puppies, explore the world with their mouth. He/she likes to chew because it calms them. But it destroys your home. Even worse – he/she might eat something like a sock that could block his/her intestines. <u>Break this habit as soon as possible</u>. If you catch your canine chewing something he/she shouldn't, you need to correct the behavior immediately. The command is "Drop It!" Commands will be discussed in further detail later on. If necessary, assist by opening their mouth and removing the object. Once the object is removed or dropped replace the object with a <u>safe</u> toy.

**"Canine's Love to chew "**      **"Provide them with Healthy Chew Toys"**

## *Begging*

There's one surefire way to prevent this: <u>Never give your canine food from the table</u>. If he/she doesn't get scraps, they <u>generally</u> won't learn to beg. Another method is to place him/*her* <u>on a leash</u> then attach the leash to a <u>door knob nearby</u> the location you are eating. Give him/her a backed bone or one of their chew toys that is scented to keep them occupied. This is called confinement without placing him/her in their crate. I like this method as it has proved to be a <u>"positive time-out"</u> for your canine.

Feeding your canine at the same time you eat, however, <u>away</u> from your eating area, will also keep him/her occupied. They should have a full stomach when they are finished eating and most likely leave them <u>less likely</u> to be interest in "your" food.

**"Wrigley, he is well trained & would never beg!"**

**"Max" well he's not begging, he just cute"**

## *Not Coming When Called*

Get into the habit of <u>praising</u> your canine when he/she comes to you, <u>whether or not you called for him/her.</u> This teaches your canine that coming to you is a "good thing". The command is "<u>COME</u>". They may not understand what you are wanting from them if you only use their name. <u>Use their name</u> to get his/her attention then command them to "<u>COME</u>".

If he/she doesn't *come,* <u>try not to chase them</u>. I know it's a human instinct to want to chase, however chasing a canine may make them want run faster and further. They may think you are playing. Call their <u>name</u> again <u>while you move</u> in the <u>opposite direction</u> (away) from him/her. This "should" make him/her <u>want to follow you</u>. If they still won't come, <u>give a different command</u> such as "<u>Sit</u>", then walk <u>slowly</u> towards him/her.

The best way to get a canine to come to you is <u>to</u> <u>lower</u> <u>your</u> <u>body,</u> <u>open</u> <u>your arms</u> then <u>call their name in an inviting voice.</u> If your canine thinks he/she is in trouble, by the negative tone in your voice, they generally will not move forward towards you. Therefore acting as though you are happy & excited to see them, may encourage him/her to want to move forward in your direction. Pour it on thick - - get happy!!!

**YES! YES! GOOD COMING!!!**

# Why Canines Bark

No one should expect a canine <u>never</u> to bark. That would be as unreasonable as expecting a child to never cry. Some canines bark excessively. If that's a problem in your home, the first step is figuring out what causes your canine to over bark. Once you know why he/she is barking, you can start to treat his/her barking issue.

Barking is one type of vocal communication that canines use, and it can mean different things depending on the situation. Here are some reasons why canines typically bark:

**Territorial/Protective:** When a person or an animal comes into an area (property/home) your canine considers their territory threatened which can often trigger excessive barking. As the threat gets closer, the barking often gets louder. Your canine will look alert and/or perhaps even look aggressive during this type of barking.

**Alarm/Fear:** Some canines bark at any noise or object that catches their attention or startles them. This can happen anywhere, not just in their home territory.

**Boredom/Loneliness:** Canines are pack animals. Canines left alone for long periods, whether in your house or in your yard, they can become bored and often will bark because they are lonely and want human interaction. Young canines should never be allowed to roam your property alone for long periods of time.

**Greeting/Play:** Canines often bark when greeting people or other animals. It's usually a happy bark, accompanied with tail wags and sometimes jumping. This is their way of saying hello.

**Attention Seeking:** Canines often bark when they want something, such as going outside, playing, or a treat.

**Separation Anxiety/Compulsive Barking:** Canines with separation anxiety often bark excessively when left alone. They also usually exhibit other symptoms as well, such as pacing, destructiveness, depression, and inappropriate elimination. Compulsive barkers seem to bark just to hear the sound of their voices. They also often make repetitive movements as well, such as running in circles, chasing their tails or running along a fence.

**"CRAZY BARKING!"**

# Typical Canine Behavior

## Potential Treatment for Excessive Barking

Getting your canine to bark less will take time, work, practice, and consistency. The command is "QUIET". As mentioned, commands will be discussed in detail later in this book. It won't happen overnight, but with proper the <u>technique</u> and <u>time</u>, you will see <u>progress</u>.

An alternative to command only, depending on the <u>reason</u> and <u>temperament</u> of your canine, might want to acquire a "No Bark Collar". You can find them on the internet and they are fairly inexpensive. I am **NOT** necessarily recommending a **No Bark "Shock Collar"**. There are many other alternatives. For example if you're canine is <u>timid in nature</u> you can try using a <u>No Bark "Spray Collar"</u>. Here is how it works. Once your canine begins to bark, they receive a warning sound, if he/she doesn't stop barking, <u>after the warning sound</u> this collar will spray citronella from under your canine's lower jaw, should he/she continue to bark. Since most canines do not like the smell or taste of citronella, they will generally stop the barking.

Another alternative is a <u>No Bark "Vibration Collars"</u>. If you canine is relentless and has a <u>somewhat territorial nature</u> however, he/she is <u>not aggressive</u> in nature, you may want to try using a No Bark Vibration Collar. It works similar to the no bark spray collar explained above however the difference is once your canine begins to bark, they will receive a warning sound, if he/she continues to bark, the consequence would be <u>vibration</u> instead of a spray. These collars generally have <u>adjustment levels</u> to adjust the intensity of the consequence. Begin on the <u>lowest</u> <u>level</u> of vibration and work your way up the levels until the barking stops.

As a last resort, you may to consider a <u>No Bark "Shock Collar"</u>. This collar is generally used when your canine is <u>aggressive in nature when barking</u>. It works similar to the vibration collar explained above, however the difference is your canine's consequence would be a <u>shock</u> instead of vibration. These collars have adjustment levels to adjust the severity of the consequence. Depending upon the <u>size</u> and <u>temperament</u> of your canine, begin on the <u>lowest</u> <u>level</u> of shock, then work your way <u>up the levels</u> until the barking stops.

If you are choosing to use a No Bark Collar, <u>I highly recommend</u> <u>leaving the collar on your canine continually</u> for a <u>minimum of 60 days</u> before attempting to see if the behavior has changed. Take the collar off only to charge it, then place it back on your canine. Should you be inconsistent with the using the collar, for example, forgetting to put it on your canine or skipping days, you will be beginning the process all over again should the behavior begin again.

# Chapter 5

## Children and New Canines

Here are some tips for you and your children. Everyone, however especially young children, should know how to treat a new canine to ensure your new pup will have a safe and happy relationship with all.

- Never leave a young child unsupervised with an animal, especially a new canine, in a new environment. Accidents can happen with the most trustworthy children and pets. Canines can get defensive when in a new environment or when a child is pulling toys from their mouth or tugging on their ears. You should not assume a young child instinctively knows how to treat an animal.
- No one, especially young children, should approach an animal, yes even your own, when he or she is eating, sleeping, chewing on a toy, in its crate or caring for its young. YOU must teach your children to distract a canine from what they are currently doing BEFORE approaching them.
- You teach your children by telling them to first using the canine's name or squeak a toy to distract them from what they are currently doing. This is to BE SURE the canine is prepared to be touched or played with. DO NOT ASSUME.
- Always pet an animal gently, with no pulling or tugging, and never from behind.
- Don't make loud noises or sudden moves when approaching an animal.
- Children should always ask an adult before approaching a canine that "you" as the child's parent, do not know.
- If an adult agrees that their canine is friendly, be sure to teach your child to reach out with the palm of their hand and gently move it forward towards the canine's nose so that he/she can smell your child.
- It is important that your child DOES NOT touch a canine's eyes, ears, nose, mouth or genitals.
- Children do not realize that animal waste is toxic and can transfer disease. Children may become curious, do not allow them to look, touch or play with animal waste.

- Do not allow your child touch a new canine or for that matter, stand near him/her during times of "heightened excitement"—for example, while a puppy/dog is eating; when someone comes to the door & your canine is overly excited, or when a canine is barking at a squirrel in the yard or perhaps at visitor through the window.

# Children and New Pets

## Stay Close to Young Children

Never assume a young child "knows" how to treat a canine if they have never been taught or have never been exposed to one!

*"Restrain your canine when a child is putting their face too close"*

**"Teach Your <u>Child</u> and Your <u>Canine</u> to be <u>GENTLE</u>"**

Children can have an enriched relation with canines when they know how to treat them.  <u>Do not assume it is instinctual for your child to know how to treat a canine</u>. Young children <u>may</u> assume a puppy is a "toy" and play too rough.  Over stimulation for a young puppy can insight unintentional however unwanted behavior.

**"Being Gentle is the Key!"**

Remember be sure that your child/children understands, any pet, young or old_ is a living, breathing creature & should be cared for and respected. Canines have needs and feelings, and they rely on us, to be their caretakers, for companionship as well as loving care.

# Chapter 6

# Knowing Your Canine's Body Language

Knowing your canine's body language can assist you in stopping unwanted behavior <u>before</u> <u>it</u> <u>begins</u>. It is <u>critical</u> to understand your canines body language especially if you think you have an aggressive canine.

## Canine Body Language

Canines are very expressive animals. They communicate when they're feeling happy, nervous, fearful and angry. They use their faces and bodies to convey much of this information. Canine body language is an <u>elaborate</u> and <u>sophisticated</u> <u>system</u> of <u>nonverbal communication</u> that, we can learn to <u>recognize</u> and <u>interpret</u>. Once you learn how to "read" your canine's postures and signals, you'll better understand his/her feelings and motivations. You will also be better able to predict what your canine is likely to do, BEFORE they do it. These skills will enable you to interact with canines with greater enjoyment and safety.

It helps to first learn about the various components that make up canine body language. Canines use facial expressions, ear set, tail carriage and overall demeanor to signal their intentions and feelings to others. Breaking their body language down into components is helpful at first for building your observation and interpretation skills. Your goal, however, is to be able to observe the entire canine and the situation or context he's in, in order to accurately determine what he's trying to say. It's not possible to understand your canine's feelings and intentions by looking at just <u>one</u> aspect of his body language. For example a wagging tail does not <u>always</u> mean your canine is happy or being friendly.

### Canine Faces

Even though canines' faces and heads come in many shapes and sizes, your canine's basic facial expressions can tell you a great deal about how they are feeling.

## "All Canines have Their Own Special Facial Expressions"

Your canine can, within limits, vary the shape and size of their eyes or the direction and intensity of their gaze. When your canine is relaxed, content and/or happy, their eyes will be their normal shape. Some canines have round eyes, while others are more almond-shaped. Eyes that appear larger than normal usually indicates that a canine is feeling threatened in some way. They may be stressed by something or they could be frightened. If you're canine's eyes seem smaller than they usually are, this can also mean he's feeling frightened or stressed. Canines who are in pain or not feeling well often look as if they're squinting their eyes. .

**GIZMO IS "CONTENT"**          **REILY IS "SMILING"**

When you know your canine well, it is easy to distinguish when he/she is smiling, happy and/or even frighten.

## Canine Hair

Although canines don't communicate much with it, you can discern some things from a canine's hair. First, a scared or stressed canine is likely to shed more than normal. It's as though the scared canine is blowing his coat, and it suddenly comes out in buckets! You may have seen this if your canine gets nervous during visits to your veterinarian. After the examination, you, the vet and the table are covered with your canine's hair.

Canines may also stick up their hair to communicate how they are, which is called "raising the hackles." Although canines' hair is most often raised over the withers (the area where the tops of a canine's shoulder blades meet); canines can also raise their hair all along their spine. Canines raise their hair when they're aroused about something. It's comparable to a person having goose bumps. Raised hackles can mean that a canine is afraid, angry, insecure, unsure, nervous or wildly excited about something.

**"Hercules is mindful ("ALERT") when someone is approaching is territory"**

## Happy, Contented

When your canine is happy, they have a **relaxed body language**. Their muscles are relaxed, the tail and ears are held in their natural positions, and they look neither large nor small for their physique. They might wag their tail from side to side or in a circular motion. Their facial expression is neutral or they appear to be happy-the muscles in their face are relaxed, the mouth is closed or slightly opened, and they might be panting with a regular tempo. The corners of his mouth (called the commissure) might be turned upwards slightly, as though they are smiling.

**"Happy & Content Canine Faces"**

## Canine Overall Body Posture

Canines also use their bodies to communicate their intentions. Usually canines either try to look normal, smaller or larger. When your canine's feeling <u>happy</u> and <u>contented,</u> he/she will look <u>normal-relaxed muscles and weight evenly balanced on all four feet</u>. Similarly, when they playful, they will look normal. They may be bouncing around or running wildly with exaggerated movements, but the facial expression and their muscles will be relaxed and nothing about his/body will look unnatural.

**"Canine Body Language Says so Much"**

## Frightened Canine

This is quite different from the overall appearance of a <u>frighten canine</u>. When your canine is frightened, <u>they will be hunched, trying to look small.</u> They might lower his body or even cower on the ground. Their head will be held low as well. If they are frightened by something or someone, they will recoil away from it. For example, if your canine is frighten on an examination table, he/she will <u>pull away from the veterinarian and lean into you or the holder.</u> If your canine is uncertain but curious about something, he/she may approach it tentatively, with their weight centered over their rear legs so that he/she can retreat quickly if needed.

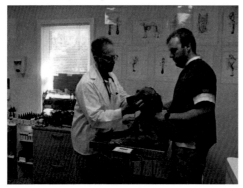

**"Loving Veterinarian"**

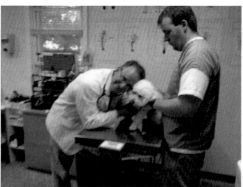

**"Frighten Canine"**

<u>A Submissive canine</u> looks very similar to a frightened canine because they make themselves look small to convey that they not a threat. If your canine is submissive, they will <u>lower their body</u> or even <u>cower on the ground.</u> His/her head might be raised, as though they are greeting a person or another animal.

**"Submissive Canines Lower Their Body to Appear Smaller"**

A dominant, alert or aroused canine tries to make themselves appear large. Their muscles will be tense. They will stand erect, sometimes even on their tiptoes, with their neck and head raised above their shoulders. Their weight will either be centered over all four feet or they will be leaning slightly forward on their front legs.

**"Be ready for anything when Your Canine has a Dominant Personality"**

An aggressive canine also makes himself/herself appear larger than life to be as intimidating as possible. If your canine is aggressive, they will look very similar to an assertive, alert or aroused canine, but their posture will be accompanied by aggressive threats. Typically, their weight will be centered over their front legs so that they can lunge or charge forward rapidly.

## Alert

When your canine is alert, <u>they may look intense and focused.</u> They stand upright with their weight centered on all fours, the ears are up and forward, and their head and neck are erect. They He hold their tail either in its natural position or vertically, possibly even over his back. The tail is rigid and immobile. Their gaze is directed toward whatever he/she has detected. The mouth is typically closed. They may growl or bark. The hair on their shoulders or back may or may not be raised.

**"Clearly Looking Intense"**

## Excited

When your canine is excited, they look as intense as they do when they are alert, <u>but they might also adopt a playful demeanor.</u> Their body is ready for action. Their look is natural in size, but their weight might be centered over their rear legs as they prepare to move. The ears are can be up and the tail is held high, and it may or may not wag. They look at the individual or object that's the source of their excitement. Excited canines often hold their mouths open, and they sometimes bark.

**"Wrigley & Noodle are Always Ready to Play"**

# Aroused

When your canine is aroused, you might have a hard time distinguishing it from when they are alert or excited. The only time it's useful to know the difference is when the arousal pushes them closer to feeling frightened or aggressive. However, just about everything else about their body language depends on whether he/she is feeling happy, scared, or uncertain. Their body may look normal-sized, the ears might be flattened to the side or held forward, and the tail might be held low, in a normal position or high. They may or may not be looking directly at an individual or object. Sometimes there's nothing in the environment that's obvious to us, but a canine can be aroused by a sound that we humans can't hear or an odor that we humans can't smell.

**"Tails Wagging"**

**"Holding On"**

**"Licking"**

# Playful

It's fairly easy to detect when your canine's feeling playful. <u>Their body movements are jerky and bouncy.</u> They might bounce around in exaggerated twists, turns and leaps. They might dodge around you, paw at you and then take off running to invite a chase. Or they might just jump on you and start mouthing. Canines enjoy a variety of play styles, including chase games (in which the canine is either the chaser or the chasee), rough-and-tumble (wrestling or tackle) games, and games of "keep-away" with an object, like a toy or stick. Almost all play is interspersed with the characteristic "play bow" that's common across all canines. When your canine play bows, he bounces into position with his forelegs on the ground and his hind legs extended so that his rear sticks up. This signal is extremely important because so much of canine play consists of aggressive behaviors and dominant postures. The play bow tells a canine's playmate, "Anything that comes after this is play, so please don't take it seriously." Some canines also show a "play face," a happy facial expression characterized by a partially open mouth that almost looks as though the canine is smiling. A playful canine might also growl or make high-pitched barks.

## "AFFECTION"

## "SILLY"

## *Fearful, Scared*

When your canine is frighten, he/she <u>does their best to look small.</u> Often, their body looks hunched, with their tail held low or tucked between their rear legs and the ears flattened back on his/her skull. They might cower close to the ground. If escape is possible, he/she might lean so that his/her center of gravity is over his rear legs to permit a hasty retreat, or lean to the side so that they can recoil. They might look directly at the source of their fear or they might look away. The muscles of their body and face are tense and rigid. They might yawn in an exaggerated way.

**LIAM is Showing "Caution"**　　　**LILY is in a "wait state"**

During interaction with a person or another canine, canines sometimes convey a confident, assertive attitude that's often called "<u>dominant</u>." If your canine is feeling dominant, their stand is tall, sometimes on their tiptoes, and tries to look large. They arch their neck. They appear tense, like a coiled spring. Their weight is squarely on all four feet or they are leaning forward slightly. The ears are up and oriented forward. The tail is high and rigid, sometimes flagging or quivering at the end. Their hair may or may not be standing up on his shoulders or along his back. They usually make direct eye contact with the other individual. They might growl, but their mouth will typically be closed.

## Submissive

If your canine is feeling submissive while they interact with a person or another canine, he/she tries to convey the underlying message that they not a threat and that aggression is unnecessary. During active submission, he/she makes their body look small by hunching over and getting low to the ground. He/she holds their tail low or tucked, sometimes rapidly wagging it back and forth. They flatten their ears or holds them off to the sides of their head. They keep their neck low to the ground, but he/she turns their muzzle up toward the other individual. They might nuzzle, lick or flick his tongue. Some canines, particularly puppies, urinate.

**"LOVINGLY SUBMISSIVE"**

## Dominant

During interaction with a person or another canine, <u>canines sometimes convey a confident, assertive attitude that's often called "dominant."</u> If your canine is feeling dominant, they stands tall, sometimes on looking like they are on their tiptoes, and tries to look large. They arch their neck. They appear tense, like a coiled spring. Their weight is squarely on all four feet or they are leaning forward slightly. The ears are up and oriented forward. The tail is high and rigid, sometimes flagging or quivering at the end. Their hair may or may not be standing up on their shoulders or along their back. They usually makes direct eye contact with the other individual. They may growl, but his mouth will typically be closed.

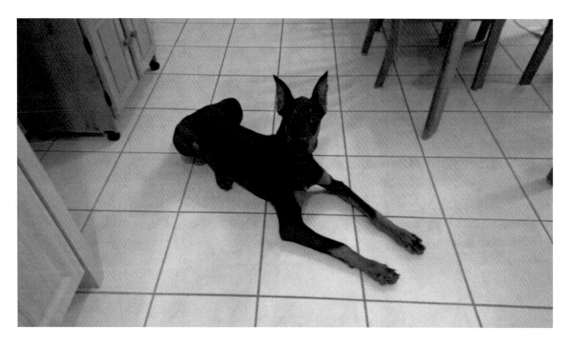

## "DOMINANT POSTURE"

# Chapter 7

## Canine Aggression

# What Is Canine Aggression?

The term "aggression" refers to a wide variety of behaviors that occur for a multitude of reasons in various circumstances. <u>Virtually all wild animals are aggressive when guarding their territories, defending their offspring and protecting themselves</u>. Species that live in packs, including people and canines, also use aggression and the threat of aggression to keep the peace and to negotiate social interactions.

To say that a canine is "aggressive" can mean a whole host of things. Aggression encompasses a range of behaviors that usually begins with warnings and can culminate in an attack. Canines may abort their efforts at any point during an aggressive encounter.

It is important to learn your canine's body language so that you can attempt to prevent aggressive behavior before it begins. Once your canine has reached a heightened state of aggression, it will be more difficult for you to control. A canine that shows aggression to people usually exhibits some part of the following sequence of increasingly intense behaviors.

- Becoming very still and rigid
- Guttural bark that sounds threatening
- Lunging forward or charging at the person with no contact
- Mouthing, as though to move or control the person, without applying significant pressure
- "Muzzle punch" (the canine literally punches the person with their nose)
- Growl
- Showing <u>teeth</u>
- Snarl (a combination of growling and showing teeth)
- Snap
- Quick nip that leaves no mark
- Quick bite that tears the <u>skin</u>
- Bite with enough pressure to cause a bruise
- Bite that causes puncture <u>wounds</u>
- Repeated bites in rapid succession
- Bite and shake

## Canine Aggression

When a canine is aggressive, they don't always follow a sequence, and they often do several of the behaviors above simultaneously. Many times, canine parents do not recognize the warning signs before a bite, so they might perceive their canines as suddenly flying off the handle. However, that's rarely the case.

It can be just <u>milliseconds</u> between a <u>warning and a bite,</u> however, it is my experience that <u>canines rarely bite without giving some type of warning beforehand.</u> This is why learning "<u>your</u>" canine's body language is so important.

**"More Than a Warning"**

If your canine has been aggressive in the past or you suspect she could become aggressive, take time to evaluate the situations that have upset him/her. Try to remember who bore the brunt of her aggression? When and where did the aggression happen? What else was going on at the time of the aggression? What happened moments before or what was about to happen to your canine when his/her aggression ensued? What seemed to stop him/her aggression? Learning the answers to these questions can clarify the circumstances that "trigger" your canine's aggressive reaction and provide insight into the reasons for his or her behavior. You need an accurate diagnosis before you can hope to help your canine.

Aggressive behavior problems in canines can be classified in different ways. A beneficial scheme for understanding why your canine is aggressive is based on the <u>function</u> or <u>purpose</u> of the aggression. If you think of aggression this way, you can determine what motivates your canine to behave aggressively and identify what he/she hopes to gain from their behavior.

# Territorial Aggression

Canines' wild relatives are territorial. They live in certain area, and they defend this area from intruders. Wolves are highly territorial. If a coyote or a wolf who's not part of a pack invades their territory, the resident wolves will attack and drive off the intruder. Some canines display the same tendencies. They bark and charge at people or other animals encroaching on their home turf. Canines are often valued for this level of territorial behavior. However, some canines will attack and bite an intruder, whether the intruder is friend or foe. Territorial aggression can occur along the boundary regularly patrolled by a canine or at the boundaries of him/her pet parents' property. Other canines show territorial aggression only toward people or other animals coming into the home. Male and female canines are equally prone to territorial aggression. Puppies are <u>rarely</u> territorial. Territorial behavior usually appears as puppies mature into adolescence or adulthood, at one to three years of age.

**"A FIGHT COULD BE BREWING"**

# Protective Aggression

Canines are usually very social species. If they were left on their own, they would live together in small packs of family and friends. If one member of a pack is in danger, the others typically rush in to help defend that individual. This is classified as protective aggression because the canines are protecting one of their own. <u>Domestic canines may show the same type of aggressive behavior when they think that one of their family members or friends (human or animal) is in peril.</u> Sometimes canines reserve protective aggression for individuals they consider particularly vulnerable. A canine who has never shown aggression to strangers in the past might start behaving aggressively when he/she has a litter of puppies. Likewise, a canine might first show protective aggression when his/her canine parents bring a new infant into the family.

While this behavior sounds appealing at first glance, problems arise when the protective canine starts to treat "everyone outside the immediate family", including friends and relatives, as threats to the baby's safety. Both male and female canines are equally prone to protective aggression. <u>Puppies are rarely protective</u>. Like territorial behavior, protective aggression usually appears as puppies mature into an adolescence or adulthood, between the ages of one to three years old.

## Possessive Aggression

Canines guard their chew bones, their toys or things they've taken without permission (stolen). Still others guard their favorite resting spots, their crates or their beds. (Often, these canines also guard their canine parents' beds!) Less common are canines who guard water bowls. Usually a possessive canine is easy to identify because they are only aggressive when they have something they want to covert. But some canines will hide their cherished toys and bones around the house and guard them from unsuspecting people or animals who have no idea that they're anywhere near a valued object. Male and female canines are equally prone to possessive aggression, and this type of aggression is common in both puppies and adults.

"THIS CANINE IS GUARDING"

70

# Fear Aggression

When animals and people are afraid, they prefer to get away from what they are afraid of. This is called the flight response. But if escaping isn't an option, most animals will switch to a fight response. They try to defend themselves from the scary thing.

So a canine can be afraid of a person or another animal but still attack if he/she thinks this is their only recourse. A fearful canine will normally adopt fearful postures and retreat, but he/she may become aggressive if cornered or trapped. Some canines will cower at the prospect of physical punishment but attack when a threatening person reaches out towards them. Fearful canines sometimes run away from a person or animal who frightens them, but if the person or animal turns to leave, they come up from behind and nip. This is why I highly suggest to avoid ever turning your back on a fearful canine. Fear aggression is characterized by rapid nips or bites because a fearful canine is motivated to bite and then run. Sometimes the aggression doesn't begin with clear threats.

### "DEFINITELY FEARFUL – A CLEAR SIGN TO STAY AWAY"

A fearful canine may show their teeth or growl to warn the victim off. In this kind of situation, the only warning is the canine's fearful posture and their attempts to retreat. Male and female canines are equally prone to fear aggression, and this type of aggression is common in both puppies and adults.

Your canine might switch from active submission to a more passive position, in which he/she lies down and rolls over on their back to display his/her inguinal area (genitalia). During passive submission, your canine might lie still, or he might paw at the other individual. They generally look away. They might whine. Some canines, particularly puppies, urinate in this position.

## Fearfully Aggressive

If your canine is fearfully aggressive they won't look any different than when they are fearful, <u>except that they might show their teeth and growl</u>. Some fearful canines never escalate to aggression, but others will if they feel there's no escape. A fearful canine isn't likely to bite a person or other animal unless all avenues for escape are blocked and he feels trapped. When this happens, they continue to cower but, at the same time, shows their teeth and might growl or snarl. If they snap or bite, it's usually lightening quickly, and then they retreats as far away from the threat as possible. Some canines wait until the person or animal who frightens them begins to retreat, and then they dart out to nip them from behind.

## Offensively Aggressive

If your canine feels anger and confidence at the same time, you might see offensively aggressive body language. They are on the attack, and he/she may or may not stop if the person or animal he's focused on stays away or retreats. They do their best to look large and intimidating by holding his/her head high, his/her ears up and forward, and his/her tail raised and rigid. They might flag their tail. The hackles might be up. They positions themselves over their forelegs so that they are ready to lunge or charge forward. They stare directly at the person or animal. They show their teeth by wrinkling their muzzle and retracting their lips vertically to display his/her front teeth.

**"ABSOLUTE SIGN OF FEAR"**

## *Defensively Aggressive*

Most canines give plenty of warning before reacting aggressively, but you need to know what to look for to recognize the signs. If your canine is feeling defensively aggressive, they would prefer <u>NOT</u> get into an altercation if they do not have to. They would rather the person or animal they are afraid of just back off and leave them alone. But at the same time, they ready to stand up for themselves. Because they are feeling both fear and anger, they often adopt a combination of fearful and offensive postures. Typically, they look large, their ears are up and forward, and the tail is held high and rigid. They center their weight squarely on all fours, over their forelegs or over their rear legs, depending on the situation.

Usually it depends on how close your canine is to the threat and whether their intention is to stand their ground, charge forward or retreat. Typically, they draw their lips back to display their teeth, and they may or may not wrinkle their muzzle. Usually they growl, snarl or bark, although the bark might be high-pitched. Often, the hackles are up. People sometimes refer to a defensively aggressive canine as adopting "a good offense as the best defense."

# "HACKELS ARE UP"

Canines like this are sometimes bluffing in that they really would not fight if push came to shove-they would likely retreat. But other canines will make the first strike, depending on the balance of confidence and fear they're feeling.

A canine whose frightened or feeling submissive probably has their mouth closed. The lips might be pulled back slightly at the corners. They might flick their tongue in and out, or they might lick if their interacting with a person or another animal. When they are feeling uptight, they might yawn in an exaggerated fashion.

# Defensively Aggressive

Some canines show a "submissive grin" when they're feeling extremely submissive. They pull their lips up vertically and display their front teeth (canines and incisors). This signal is almost always accompanied by an overall submissive body posture, such as a lowered head, yelping or whining, and squinty eyes. Only some canines "grin" this way. People sometimes mistakenly think a canine is being aggressive when, in fact, grinning submissively and trying to communicate the exact opposite of aggression.

A canine who's signaling their intention to act aggressively will often retract their lips to expose their teeth. They may pull their lips up vertically to display their front teeth while also wrinkling the top of the muzzle. This is typical of a canine who's warning you not to come any closer.

**"RETRACTING LIPS"**

A canine may draw their lips back horizontally so that the lips are really tight at the commissure (the corners of the mouth). With this expression, you're more likely to see both the front and back teeth (premolars and molars). This posture is often indicative of a canine who's feeling afraid. However, once a canine is ready to bite, they usually <u>pull their lips</u> up <u>AND</u> <u>back</u> so that their <u>mouth is open</u> and <u>teeth are exposed</u>.

## Food Guarding – (Classified as Possessive Aggression)

Canines evolved from wild ancestors who had to compete for food, nesting sites and mates to survive. Even though our domestic canines no longer face such harsh realities, many still show the tendency to guard their possessions from others, whether they need to or not. Some canines only care about their food. These canines might react aggressively when a person or another animal comes near their food or approaches them while they're eating, especially when they are on a lead holding them back from protecting their food.

## "FOOD GUARDING"

## Exercises for Food Guarding

The exercises used for food guarding are desensitization combined with counter conditioning. They're highly effective but fairly complex and detailed. If you have a sense of fear when your canine begins to guard their food, I highly suggest you hire a Professional Canine Trainer to assist you with this issue. Your canine will easily pick up on your fear and that could make the following exercise very dangerous.

The exercises described below are done in stages. After doing the exercises in one stage, you can progress to the next stage if your canine is relaxed and shows no signs of aggression. Canine body language can be complex, so it's sometimes difficult to tell how a canine feels at any given moment. To determine what your canine looks like when he's relaxed, take note of what their body, ears, eyes and tail do when you know they are in a situation they find pleasant.

## Exercises for Food Guarding

For example, notice what your canine looks like when you and he are relaxing together on the couch or taking a leisurely walk. Signs that a canine feels calm and content include a relaxed posture (muscles relaxed, not tensed), normal breathing or slight panting, eating at a normal pace, wagging and wiggling.

**"SARGENT IS THE BEST EXAMPLE OF A DOG WHO IS <u>NOT</u> GUARDING FOOD"**

Some signs of aggression to watch for as you're doing exercises include standing stiffly over the bowl, gulping the food, tensing or freezing, growling, staring, snapping, & snarling.

# GROWL   SNARL

# Exercises for Food Guarding

## Phase I

- Stand a few feet away from your canine while he eats dry kibble from a bowl on the floor. <u>Do not move toward your canine.</u>
- Say something like, "Hey, what have you got there?" <u>in a conversational tone</u> and, <u>at the same time</u>, toss a "special" treat toward the bowl. USE A <u>NEW</u> TASTY (STRONG SMELLING) TREAT THAT <u>YOU HAVE TESTED</u> WITH YOUR CANINE (PRIOR) TO YOU CAN BE SURE IT WILL GET HIS/HER ATTENTION. <u>Continue to do this every few seconds until your canine finishes eating his kibble.</u>
- Repeat this exercise each time you feed your canine until he <u>eats in a relaxed way</u> for <u>10 meals in a row.</u> Then you can move on to Stage Two.
- During your exercises, should your canine leave the bowl and move toward you to ask for more treats, <u>IGNORE</u> him/her. Wait until he/she goes back to his/her bowl and starts eating again before tossing more treats.

## Phase II

- While your canine eats dry kibble from a bowl on the floor, say "Hey, what have you got there?" <u>in a conversational tone</u>. At the same time, <u>take one step toward him/her</u> and toss <u>THE NEW TREAT</u> towards the bowl. <u>Immediately</u> <u>step back</u>. Repeat this sequence every few seconds until your canine has finished eating.
- <u>Each day,</u> <u>take one step closer</u> to your canine <u>before tossing THE NEW TREAT.</u> Continue at this stage <u>until you come within two feet of the bowl.</u> When your canine eats in a <u>relaxed way for 10 meals in a row</u> as you repeatedly approach and stand two feet away and give him a treat, you're ready to move to the next stage.

## Phase III

- While your canine eats dry kibble from a bowl on the floor, approach him saying "Hey, what have you got there?" <u>in a conversational tone</u>. <u>Stand next to your canine's bowl</u> and <u>drop THE NEW TREAT into bowl.</u> Then <u>immediately turn around and walk away.</u>
- Repeat the sequence every few seconds until your canine has finished eating. When your canine eats in a <u>relaxed way for 10 meals in a row,</u> you're ready for the next stage.

# Phases for Food Guarding Exercises

## Phase IV

- While your canine eats dry kibble from a bowl on the floor, approach him saying "Hey, what have you got there?" _in a conversational tone_. _Stand next to your canine_, holding _THE NEW TREAT_ in your hand. _Bend down slightly_, holding the treat out _just an inch or two_ in your canine's direction. _Encourage him to stop eating_ the food in the bowl to take _THE NEW TREAT. After your canine eats the treat from your hand, immediately turn around and walk away._ Repeat this sequence _every few seconds_ until your canine has finished eating.
- _Each day, bend down a little more_ when you offer your canine _THE NEW TREAT_ so that your _hand moves an inch or two closer_ to his bowl. Stay at this stage _until you can bend down and hold your hand with THE NEW TREAT right next to your canine's bowl._ When your canine eats _relaxed for 10 meals in a row as you repeatedly approach_ to _bend down and offer him a treat next to his bowl,_ you're ready for the next stage.

## Phase V

- While your canine eats dry kibble from a bowl on the floor, approach him saying "Hey, what have you got there?" _in a conversational tone_. Stand next to your canine, bend down and touch his bowl with one hand while offering him a _THE NEW TREAT_ with your other hand.
- Continue to do this every few seconds until your canine has finished the food in his bowl. _When your canine eats relaxed for 10 meals in a row,_ you can move to the next stage.

## Phase VI

- While your canine eats dry kibble from a bowl on the floor, approach him saying "Hey, what have you got there?" _in a conversational tone_. Stand next to your canine, bend and pick up his bowl with one hand. _Raise it only six inches off the floor_ and drop _THE NEW TREAT in the bowl_. Then _immediately return_ the _bowl_ to the _floor_ so that your canine can eat from it.
- Continue to do this every few seconds until your canine has finished all the food in his bowl. _As you repeat the sequence, raise the bowl slightly higher off the floor each time until you can lift it all the way up to your waist and stand upright._

- Repeat the sequence, _this time, when you pick up your canine's bowl, walk over to a table or counter with it._ Then put _THE NEW TREAT into the bowl,_ walk back to your canine and _return the bowl to the same place on the floor._

*Phase VII: Making It Work for Everyone*

- The last stage is to have <u>all ADULT family members</u> go through stages one through six. <u>Each person</u> needs to <u>start at the beginning</u> and progress <u>through</u> the <u>steps the same way,</u> always making sure that your canine continues to look relaxed and comfortable during exercises. <u>DO NOT assume</u> that because your canine is okay with <u>one person approaching</u> the bowl, they will <u>automatically be comfortable</u> with another <u>person doing the same thing.</u> Your canine has to <u>learn</u> that the rules work the same way <u>with everyone.</u>
- The entire treatment program is <u>gradual enough to</u> help your canine relax and anticipate the "special treats" rather than feel threatened and become aggressive when people approach him while he/she is eating. Through the exercises, your canine will learn that people approaching their food bowl <u>bring even tastier food</u>—people are not coming to take his/her food away.
- Apart from your treatment sessions, <u>"YOU"</u> need to manage your canine's behavior carefully to avoid aggressive encounters. <u>Do not</u> allow others to go close to your canine while eating. If your canine guards food from children in the family, <u>DO NOT attempt these exercises with any child under 18 years of age</u>

# Managing Your Canine's Behavior

If your canine guards food from visitors to your home, it might be easier to manage his behavior BEFORE resolving it. <u>If your canine and guests are in the same room, remove all food items from the area.</u> Alternatively, you should keep your canine confined in his/her crate while guests visit. Be aware that canines sometimes guard food intended for people, even if the food is situated on a table or countertop. <u>If food is going to be present when guests visit, you'll want to confine your canine to ensure everyone's safety.</u>

# What NOT to Do

- <u>Do not "free feed"</u> your canine (leave out bowls of food all the time). If your canine guards food, he/she should not have constant access to it. <u>Only feed your canine meals at regularly scheduled times.</u>
- <u>Do not punish or intimidate your canine when he guards food.</u> Remember that when a person approaches a food-guarding canine, the canine <u>will react</u> as though the person intends to take the food away. This makes sense because canines naturally compete for food.
- <u>It's easier and safer to simply change the way your canine feels about people approaching him when they have food through desensitization and counterconditioning.</u> Be patient. <u>Desensitization takes time</u>. <u>DO NOT</u> rush through the phases. It may take a family member longer to get through the phases. It is worth the wait.

# Chapter 8

# *Humans – Are a Chatty Culture*
## Canine's – Not so Much

NON-VERBAL COMMUNIATION

SPEAKS LOUDLY

**"Using Your Body Language when Communicating
with Your Canine is Much More Effective"**

## Human Body Language

What canines rely on <u>MOST</u> to figure out what the desired behavior a humans wants is <u>our body language</u>. Canines have evolved to be expert readers of the human body language and they can quickly figure out the behavior you desire <u>before</u> you say the words by watching your facial expressions and body language. Hence we can easily send mixed messages if we are only paying attention to what we are saying with our mouth when we are not paying attention to the movement of our physical bodies. Try visiting any canine beginners training class, you will see plenty of humans saying one thing, doing another thing with their body language and confused canines when they are trying to figure out what in the world is going on.

## "Hmm, Let Me See What these Humans are "<u>trying</u>" to Say"

The human species is a very vocal (chatty) culture. We love to chatter away, particularly with our canines. Nonetheless your canine most likely does not understand the vast majority of what you are saying. Canines are able to connect a few key words from repetition. Most of the time, young canines <u>cannot process a lot words</u> all at one time. More often than not, the more words you speak, the more confused your canine can become. In most cases, canines consider human chatter - - PRAISE.

## Human Body Language

Think about it, young canines are able to put together *a* few key words so when we speak quickly, using lots of words and his/her name... your canine is hearing "their name", then lots of mumbo jumbo after it. For example when you teach "come" <u>your body</u>, most likely, is remaining "still" however you are repeating a movement command "COME!" Meaning you want him/her to move. Your canine is not moving towards you, because "your body" is remaining still. We become annoyed with our canines and start correcting them by speaking quickly with something like: "Duke get over here right now! What your canine hearing? "Duke Blah – blah –blah. They simply cannot process all the words you are speaking when you are speaking so quickly and therefore he/she is unsure of the desired behavior.

The correct way of expressing a command or recall is by giving a command in a strong – slow – assertive voice. When using more than two words, make your voice sound robotic, for instance: "Duke (Using your canine's name to get his /her attention) - - Come (move your body) – - Here (pointing to your side) - - Now (voice firm)" (matching your body language to the command).

## Human Body Language

A good example is when first teaching your canine to "Stay". The desired behavior is that <u>your canine's body remains still</u>, yet often times, we raise our hand, command "STAY", as <u>WE move away 'from our canines.</u> Your body language is inviting your canine to move forward toward you! A canine will instinctively want follow your feet. You need to realize that it takes time and practice to add Distance, Duration and Distractions. <u>Professionally know as the 3 "D's".</u> Usually it can take anywhere from 2 to 6 weeks BEFORE you can add the 3"D's" to a command OR you at least need to wait until you canine is proficient in the command. (Remaining still before adding distraction)

**"BEGIN WITH "YOUR" BODY STILL"**   **"WHEN YOU PUP IS READY – BEGIN TO MOVE"**

When first beginning to teach "STAY" <u>YOUR body</u> needs to remain still, moving only your hand, in a <u>slow, upward, then downward direction</u>, repeating "<u>STAY</u> ". <u>Keep your canines eyes focused on "your hand".</u> When beginning to move your hand, <u>should your canine look down at your feet,</u> snap your fingers or make noise with your mouth, to <u>bring their attention back to your hand.</u> After a short time after practicing "STAY" with <u>YOUR</u> body <u>remaining still,</u> when your canine is properly focused on your hand & not your feet, you can begin to <u>SLOWLY MOVE AWAY</u> from your canine. At this point he/she is ready to remain still (for a short period of time). Time will extend with more practice.

# Human Body Language

As I have mentioned, canines are experts at reading your body language and listening to the tone of our voice. When you "<u>SAY</u>" one thing with your mouth however your body language is doing something different, your canine becomes confused. They may "shut down" & just look at you aimlessly.

Using Leading Edge Hand Commands provides an easier method of teaching your canine commands. You will find your canine can learn command & desired behavior up to <u>4 times faster</u> by simply <u>using the correct human body language</u> when you are teaching them. We will discuss Leading Edge Hand Commands, in further detail in an upcoming chapter.

## THEY ARE ALL IN A "WAIT STATE" FOLLOWING MY BODY LANGUAGE WHEN THE DOORBEL IS RINGING

# Chapter 9

## Training Techniques

There are many different training techniques in the canine training industry today. We will discuss two (2) of them. The traditional "Break Training" technique and my new "Break -Through Training" technique. I am certified in both training however, whenever possible, I choose "Break –Through" Training.

There are lots of opinions regarding Positive Reinforcement Techniques and Negative Reinforcement Techniques. I believe that unnecessary negative reinforcement can & usually does breed fear. Fear causes unpredictable behavior and can sometimes be the result of aggressive behavior. The results can be devastating. This is just a few examples of negative behaviors that fear can trigger: biting without warning, destroying your property and barking incessantly.

## What is the Typical "BREAK- TRAINING" Technique?

"Break" training has been around for many years. When using this type of training strict corrections are enforced to teach a puppy or older canine wanted behaviors. The word "NO" is frequently used without stating the unwanted behavior and the demand for respect from canine to the human is usually acquired by using excessive force and harsh corrections. When a canine does not listen, the trainer loudly yells the word NO! Tugs hard on the lead to bring the canine into submission. In some cases, when teaching an aggressive canine, this training technique may prove to be effective.

# What is My New "BREAK - THROUGH TRAINING" Technique?

My new "Break-Through" training is a method I have designed by which a trainer, handler or owner who has taken this course information "teaches" wanted behavior by using human body language, voice techniques, scent and proper positive reinforcement techniques BEFORE issuing consequence. Each of the bullets below will be explained in further detail later.

- Teaches focus – A focused canine is the key to success with any training.
- Uses scent which activates the mucus membranes in the canine nose then allows the canine brain to move forward into learning mode.
- Uses "YOUR "body language for simple interpretation of your expectation to your canine
- Use voice recognition (positive or negative) your voice must match the command or correction.
- Establishes the Alpha – Canines are Pack Animals & Pack members need a hierarchy
- Uses proper timing for correction and praise - be in his/her moment
- Proper Positive Reinforcement - proper praise method to reinforce wanted behavior.
- Correction when necessary - proper correction method when you say "NO" say "WHY"
- The younger the canine, the shorter period of time when working commands
- Distance, duration & distraction are added slowly at the appropriate time, when your canine is ready
- Work sheets for easy work time – each command will be written out – step by step - in the following chapters. Use the written commands as work sheets to practice commands with your canine.
- Always begin working training commands ON LEAD – the lead provides you with the control you need when necessary.
- Continued practice, using this training method with your everyday events. It is crucial to practice, even when you think your canine knows the commands. It creates a sharp canine mind.

*Chapter 10*

*Rules of Engagement for Canine Training*

# What are Commands?
# Commands are NOT

- Commands <u>ARE NOT</u> requests, questions or songs.  Use a <u>firm, assertive voice</u>.
- Work your canine <u>ON THE LEAD</u>, even if you do not touch it.
- Your <u>body language</u> <u>NEEDS</u> to <u>match the command.</u>
- Use <u>Leading Edge Hand Commands</u> with <u>BOTH</u> <u>Commands</u> and <u>Praise</u>
- Use scent to <u>activate the canine brain</u> /be inconsistent when releasing treats)
- Once your canine knows the command, use your body language to <u>guide</u> your canine into the command.
-  Repeating a command conditions your canine <u>NOT</u> to listen <u>the first time</u> he/she is commanded. They are waiting for you to say the command again in a serious assertive tone.  Be patient. <u>Wait it out!</u>  Once YOU KNOW your canine "knows" a command, use your body language to express the wanted behavior.

IMPORTANT NOTE:  Praise equals the following:
Use the word - <u>YES</u> (To <u>agree</u> with the wanted behavior - <u>immediately</u>)
Use the word – <u>Good</u> (Good confirms agreement with wanted behavior)
Use the <u>Command</u> (Using the command teaches your canine "<u>WHY</u>" they are good)

**Example:  Yes! Good Looking!**

# Rules of Engagement for Canine Training

*Don't Over Work It*

Over working your canine, especially when they are very young, can be counterproductive. After years of experience, it is my professional opinion that working canines, especially the younger ones, in shorter increments of time, has proven to be much more effective. There is a very practical reason for this. The young canine mind is a simple mind and <u>requires time to process information.</u> The younger the canine, the more time they need to process what you are saying & your body language.

When canines are older, they have may have established some bad habits, therefore changing their behavior takes time and additional practice. Either way <u>small increments of time</u>, with <u>repetition</u> of one and two word commands works more efficiently. You want your canine to be <u>relaxed</u> not stressed after completing a training session with you

Much like preschool aged children, your canine's brain cannot process a lot of information, all at once. Whether your canine is learning a new process/commands for the first time or your canine needs to change unwanted behavior- unless the "<u>act</u>" or "<u>command</u>" is <u>instinctual</u> to your canine, it will requires <u>time to process</u> the information. Practicing in <u>small increments of time</u> with <u>repetitive words</u> is key. You will find it is best to start with short increments of time, adding time and additional training sessions according to your canine's ability to process information. If you are training correctly, your canine will be in a <u>relaxed</u> state of mind after a training session.

## Reeses & Snickers      Jack & Shyla
**"After a training session, they were all completely relaxed"**

## Rules of Engagement for Canine Training

There are times when bringing a professional canine trainer into your home will prove helpful. When a trainer comes to your home, they bring a different energy to your canine. Similar to a young pre-school child, canines will act differently in front of his/her trainer as a child would act differently when in front of his/her teacher. I often am asked "why a pup will work <u>better for me</u> then their owner?" The answer is often, humans make training complicated. When a human does not understand how the canine brain works, we are viewed, by a canine, as an unstable energy. If your energy is unstable, your canine will react in an unstable manor. However, <u>you</u>, as a canine parent, <u>using the right methods & techniques</u>, will become <u>pack leader.</u> Using the correct tools, you will be able to teach your canine more than you can imagine.

## "BAILEY & DONNA"

# Chapter 11

## ONE MINUTE Training Session Time Line: By Canine Age

1. **ONE MINUTE Training Sessions**:

   For optimum results, when using this program, it is important that you realize that your canine's brain is similar to a human toddler's brain. The younger the canine, the more simple they think. When your canine is young, they are easily distracted. Since your canine is unable to process a lot of information at one time, he/she will work best & be able to stay more focused when you work commands in small increments of time. This enables your canine to retain more information. Working commands in **small increments** of time, numerous times daily is most effective. Take a look at the following canine age to daily session time schedule.

   **Age: 8 to 12 weeks**: Suggested work time: <u>ONE</u> minute increments of time. "Work" commands minimally <u>4 to 5 times a day</u>. For every 3 to 4 weeks of completed training add <u>ONE</u> additional minute to each training sessions. No more than 5 minutes per session – 4 to 5 sessions per day.

   **Age: 13 to 20 weeks:** If there has been no prior formal training, I recommend you begin "working command" in <u>ONE</u> minute increments. Add 1 to 2 additional daily sessions. At this age you will be "working command" with your canine 6 to 7 times a day, in ONE minute increments. For every 3 to 4 weeks of completed training add <u>ONE</u> additional minute to each training sessions. No more than 5 minutes per session up to 5 to 6 sessions per day.

   **Age: 6 to 8 Months:** If there has been no prior formal training, begin with <u>ONE</u> minute sessions, adding additional minutes (one minute at a time) and <u>additional sessions</u> only <u>after</u> you are able to determine <u>your canine is progressing</u>. It is not recommended that you "work command" with your canine for more than 15 minutes per session, in any given training session when they are *under 1 year of age.* No more than 15 minutes per session – maximum of 6 to 8 sessions per day or as tolerated.

   **9 Months to 1 Year of age:** Begin working <u>ONE</u> minute <u>training sessions</u> for <u>one week</u>. This will condition your canine to the expected behavior during a training session. Your canine is *most likely* more mature and should be able to adjust to additional work time & additional sessions quickly. Add <u>ONE</u> minute to each session as you see his/her "<u>focus</u>" begin to increase. Maximum 15 minutes "work time" per session per day. The amount of sessions should be as tolerated by your canine.

## Rules of Engagement for Canine Training

**1 Year of age +**: Remember, this is <u>beginner's training</u>. Therefore even with older canines, <u>15 minute training sessions</u>, as you see fit, according to your canine's ability to focus. The more often your "work command" with your canine, the sharper your canine will become. However regardless of your canine's age, you must take into consideration your canine's maturity & his/her ability to focus. When you are "correcting" your canine often, your canine is not ready for extended the amount of time in a session. Make your sessions shorter and work less sessions.

**"Rocky – Donna - Sheena"**

# "Training 1 or 4 Canines ...

# Anything is Possible When <u>You</u> Work it!"

## Reasons for Canine Training

Training, especially for a young canine, is important for many reasons. Here are just a few.

- It keeps your canine safe.
- It ensures your canine will not adopt unwanted behaviors for example: Pulling on the leash, jumping and begging during dinner, & <u>destructive tendencies</u>.
- It can provide your canine the structure he/she desires, direction and expectations which make them feel secure.
- Training also provides you and your canine quality time and a positive owner/ canine relationship.
- Whether your canine is young or old, large or small, calm or hyper, whatever behavior you allow in the beginning will be the behavior you and your canine will live with for the life of your canine.
- Training can be a positive step toward lifelong dog and owner happiness. However it will only work when <u>you</u> work it. Your canine can learn, however your consistency and your follow up creates the sharp canine you desire.

**"DONNA & PIPPA"**

# Rules of Engagement for Canine Training

      Once your initial training is complete, you should <u>continue to work with your canine on a daily basis</u>. Your training sessions will increase in time as your canine is able to stay focused for longer periods of time. Practice, practice, practice...although <u>you</u> will most likely never achieve perfection, animals will inevitably make mistakes from time to time, the amount of time <u>you</u> work with your canine will clearly make the difference when it comes to his/her behavior and how long they take to "get it".

      As "human parents" we sing the ABC's for a very long time. We constantly taught our human children "A" is for "apple" and so on. We didn't have the expectation that our human child would read before learning all the ABC's. It took a long time to draw out the sounds and then the words etc. however long it took, we remained patient knowing the end results would come. The same concept applies to our canines.

**"DONNA & BUDDY"**     **"DONNA & BAILEY"**     **DONNA & PATRICK"**

# Helpful Suggestions

Exercise-Discipline-Affection
Energy, Instinct & Emotions

Keep it Simple
Be Committed
One Minute at a Time
Work Commands Dailey

Say What <u>You</u> Mean
Mean What <u>You</u> Say
Don't Say it Meanly

It's Not Just Training, It's a Lifestyle
Short Calm Assertive Commands
Firm Assertive Corrections
Positive Reinforcement
Praise & Affection

# Chapter 12

# *12 Steps to Success*

**"ROCKY & DONNA"**

## 12 Steps to Success

1.  Lead on - Wait for Calm:

    Most <u>humans</u> become overly excited when getting ready to place a collar & lead on their canines.  Humans start the excitement early on in the process by using "lots of high pitched words" and "very upbeat energy". Hence, before you can even get the collar & lead out of the draw, while you are walking to the collar/leash spot, YOU are literally coaching your canine to become more and more excited.  Sound familiar?

    Humans usually put the collar and lead on their canines while they are still over stimulating them.  We "psych out" our canine with unnecessary (words) conversation. We say things like: Come On!  Let's go! Want to go outside? At this time continuing to chat with our canines very counterproductive.  By this time your canine is so <u>mentally over stimulated</u> they can hardly contain themselves.

    We all do it or should I say, have done it!  "We" are "conditioned" to associate the lead with excitement.  Then of course "OUR" human expectation, for these very simple minded, instinctual, canines...is that they will "just know" sit down and allow us to calmly put the lead on. **Nope..... _WRONG!_**

**NO FOCUS HERE!**

# *12 Steps to Success*

2.  Lead on - Wait for Calm continued:

Your canine needs to learn how to be calm on the lead.  It is a state of mind that to a young canine, does not come naturally most of the time.  It is up to you to provide the calm energy it takes to begin a training session.   It is important when first beginning to train your canine using the lead. Even though your canine may have previous training knowledge, the lead will provide you with leadership and control.  DO NOT begin your ONE minute training session if your canine is in an overly excited frame of mind.

## LEASH ON – WAIT FOR CALM

## 12 Steps to Success

3. Suggestions on how to begin to calm your canine when they see the leash/lead.

- From this point forward we will refer to the leash as "<u>A LEAD</u>". Trainers use a lead as a primary tool. It is important to disassociate your canine's lead with any form of excitement. Simply by holding the lead over your canine's head implies leadership to your canine. You are becoming the pack leader in your canine's world.

- Take the lead out often, just place it on the coffee table, sofa etc. Allow your canine to smell the lead and get familiar with the fact that the lead does not mean they are going outside. Do not have a discussion with your canine about the lead or why it is there. Do not allow your canine to play with the lead. When your canine reaches a calm state of mind, put the lead away. Continue to take the lead out often and <u>say nothing</u>. This will condition your canine that the lead is a tool. They will eventually disassociate the lead with excitement because the lead is in their view more often & you are not inviting them to go outside (for a walk) whenever they see it.
- Should your canine continue to become so overly excited when he/she sees the lead, it may be helpful for you to take a stronger approach. Place the lead on your canine, put the lead to the floor and step on it with your foot. Leave <u>very little room</u> from your canine's collar to your foot (perhaps a foot). Your canine will fuss for a time, but after he/she has tuckered themselves out, realizing that he/she cannot jump and you are ignoring their excitement, they will surrender. It takes a fairly short period of time. Do not look, talk or touch your canine until they are calm.

# *12 Steps to Success*

## Why do I have to use a Lead?

- Both <u>you and your canine</u> need to be in <u>a calm state of mind</u> before beginning a training session. Calm energy will provide your canine with the focus & stability he/she will need to learn. A calm state of mind places you in a stable mindset & a leadership position.

- By using the lead (every time) when beginning a training session, you are conditioning your canine that a training session is "work" time. The lead will provide the control you need, to guide your canine through working commands and will prevent your canine from walking away when he/she desires. Once again, the lead places you in a leadership status.

- It may take some time to condition you canine that <u>the lead is a tool</u>, not a toy that is associated with going outside. The lead will take on a new meaning of calm state of mind & work time. In addition, your canine will begin to have a new found respect for <u>YOU</u> as a leader.

4. Begin **EVERY** training session with: FOCUS- command "**LOOK**"

- The first command your canine needs to learn is eye to eye contact. Better known as focus. The command is called "LOOK". When your canine is "LOOKING" at you he/she is beginning to understand focus. Once focused, your canine will read your body language and listen more efficiently to your tone of voice.

- Focus is the key to success with any type of training. Whether you are teaching basic obedience, agility, security training, etc., without focus, it will be difficult at best to obtain a high level of success.

- Focus will make your training sessions successful. Repeat the "LOOK" command as often as necessary. When your canine is already looking at you and appears to be focused, praise the behavior! YES GOOD LOOKING!

5. How to properly COMMAND your canine.
   - Match your body language to your voice. Use Leading Edge Hand Commands.
   - Commands are NOT questions, requests or songs. When you "ask" or extend the command by "singing" the word, your canine will commonly not respond sharply. Example: Siiiiit???
   - Commands = <u>Calm, Assertive Voice</u>. Keep your voice steady & firm. This does not imply that you should be yelling at your canine. This implies your voice should be <u>FIRM.</u>
   - There are times when you can say ONE word which will simply interrupt unwanted behavior such as HEY! Or making a noise such as a loud clap of your hands - will startle you young canine and they may stop whatever they are doing. At this point, since you have not given a direct command, Good boy/girl would apply.

# 12 Steps to Success

6. How to properly PRAISE your canine.

- When you praise your canine it is important to "SAY WHY" he or she is good. (Why = Wanted behavior)
- Praise = Yes + Good + Command Used
- By using the word YES, your young canine begins to build self-esteem. They become proud of themselves and begins to understand they are doing something correctly. Canines are people pleasers and some desperately want your approval.
- The statement "good boy/good girl" when said by itself, is "general". We humans say "good b/girl" to everything a young canines does. Canines need to be taught, repetitively, why he/she is good.
- Most young canines associate the words Good Boy/Girl with a reward (treat) they do not relate it to or with a command unless you are repeatedly saying why they are "good".
- When you say good boy/girl to *EVERYTHING* your young canine does, the statement loses its praise value.
- Use Good boy/girl to extend positive reinforcement of a command or action.

7. How You Praise Matters:

Upbeat Voice Praise:
- In most cases canine parents want praise with upbeat high pitched voice, showing approval & excitement for acceptable behavior. If your canine does not over react or pop-out of the command, this is completely acceptable. Placing an "ING" or "ES" at the end of a (word) command, whenever possible, can also be very helpful. Your voice will adjust to a higher pitch and your canine will instinctively understand they have done something correctly. For Example: YES! GOOD! SITTING!

# 12 Steps to Success

Praise Matters continued

Monotone praise:

- Many young canines become overly excited when your voice pitch is too high and/or upbeat, causing him/her to pop out of the command. In such cases Monotone Praise is suggested. Keep your voice in a Low & Steady tone, perhaps adding a "growl" to your tone. This is especially important when you are attempting to keep your canine in a "still command" such as "WAIT" or "STAY" Your body language should be fairly still or moving slowly to match calm and/or still behavior wanted.
- Keeping your voice in a low tone and if possible, add a little "growl" effect to your voice. The growl effect implies in an Alpha way, you are in agreement with the behavior.

8. How to properly CORRECT your canine.
   - There is a distinct difference between yelling at your canine and using a Firm Voice when correcting. Having a Firm Voice does not imply negative energy to your canine. It implies a level of seriousness to your voice that your canine can clearly relate to.
   - Should you find yourself yelling when correcting your canine, notice your canine's body language. They will pick up on the negative energy. His/her ears may go down or back. Their body language is telling you your canine does not understanding what you want furthermore they are now afraid and insecure.
   - When you SAY "NO" - - SAY WHY. Stating the unwanted behavior teaches your canine the unacceptable behavior. For example NO! OFF! This reinforces the unwanted behavior of jumping.
   - When you constantly using the word NO without stating "why", the word NO, loses its intended value. After all - - Everything is "NO" when your canine is young and does not understand the behavior you are wanting.
   - The key is to always follow through when correcting your canine, with positive reinforcement once your canine complies with the correction.
   - "Yes! Good Off" – Good Boy!
   - DO NOT end a training session with a correction. Not only would this be showing attention to unwanted behavior, it will discourage your canine from wanting to work in the future.

Note: There will be times when the word NO or Hey will be enough said....as your canine will read your body language and know exactly the undesired behavior. And yes, there will be times when silence is golden.

# 12 Steps to Success

9. The Purpose of using Scent (treats).

- The purpose of using scent is to <u>activate the mucus membranes in your canine's nose.</u> This activation <u>allows the canine brain to move forward</u> into a learning mode. When the mucus membranes in a canine's nose are activated, your canine brain is able to move forward then he/she will be able to focus and follow your body language.
- Hold the scent in between your first 2 fingers then begin to give your canine multiple commands before releasing it. Before you know it your canine will be doing two, three, four commands before receiving reward.
- Always reward on "<u>your</u>" command. Most canine's will follow the scent and will begin to "work "meaning "follow" your commands very swiftly once you have activated their nose and incentivized them with reward. In the same way, if your canine "sits" before "<u>you</u>" command him/her to sit, <u>verbally praise</u> (yes good sitting) then <u>verbally provide another command</u>, such as down, BEFORE <u>releasing the treat.</u> Now you are releasing the scent on <u>YOUR command</u>, not on "their" Sit.
- Your goal is not only "<u>One time listening</u>", it is "One time listening on <u>YOUR command.</u>" Puppies and older dogs are smarter than you realize, though simple minded, they may learn your routine quickly, if you reward them on the same command every time, or on every completed command, they will not work unless they are given reward. In the same way, when he/she is going into the next anticipated command, before you have said the command or given the leading edge hand command, verbally praise them. However only release the treat when <u>you</u> have <u>issued</u> the <u>command.</u> Simply praise & give another command. Make it <u>your training</u> - not your canines exercise for food.
- Some canines are extremely food motivated. You want them to "<u>FOCUS</u>" and "<u>work commands</u>" because <u>YOU are pack leader</u>. You do <u>NOT</u> want your canine <u>working for the food factor</u>.
- Eventually you will be fading out scent (treats) and you will primarily use praise & affection. It takes time and practice.

Note: It takes time and practice before your canine will work commands for praise only. Remember be <u>inconsistent</u> when <u>releasing</u> the <u>scent</u> (treat)

# 12 Steps to Success

Praise - When You Are Assisting Your Canine:

- When first beginning a new training process, especially when working with a young canine, you will most likely need to assist your canine by using your hands or the lead etc., even though assistance is needed, positive reinforce the command as the goal was still achieved.

- Example: You command your canine to sit, he/she needed assistance with the command so you placed your hand on his/her lower back and assisted them into the sit position. You should still praise. Yes! Good Sitting, Good Boy! Be sure to use the Leading Edge Hand Commands with praise.

10. How to End Your Training Sessions:

- ALWAYS end your session on a POSITIVE note.
- DO NOT end your training session on a correction. If after a few moments, you realize you are re-commanding and correcting more than praising, your canine is simple not focused.
- STOP the training session HOWEVER before doing so, look for a reason to praise.
- For example: If your canine sits instantly, on the first command, then use the sit command and praise. Even though your pup was not focused and you ended your session early.... you have ended on a positive note.
- After some time has passed, begin your training session again.

## *12 Steps to Success*

11. "It works if "YOU" work it!"

- The ONE Minute Dog Trainer Program only when you are committed to working the program and working continually with your canine.
- "YOU" must consistently work your canine, even though you think he/she knows the commands. Practice, practice, practice.
- It is highly suggested that you pre-schedule session time to work with your canine daily.
- Once you have completed all the commands, your canine will be trained according to his/her ability to learn. More importantly, they will be trained according to YOUR ability to keep your canine focused & motivated as the months move forward.
- To maintain & improve your canines' level of knowledge & focus while working command and to create a sharply trained canine, it is recommended that YOU continue to work commands (with your canine) ON LEAD, every day for a minimum of 3 to 6 months after completing the initial training.
- "Knowing" command and "being proficient" in command are completely different. You must to continue to place your canine on the lead and work commands with him/her daily, to improve their skills, knowledge and response time.

# Chapter 13

## *Focus Can Make all the Difference*

## "HARLEY & DONNA"

## Focus is the Foundation

Here is where you will learn how to teach your canine to focus. Without true focus, canine training can be difficult at best. No matter what type of training you may be teaching, agility training, standard obedience or even security training, the more focused the canine, the more they are able to learn in a shorter period of time.

You are the key to your canine's success when you will learn how to develop your canine's focus. When your canine is giving you eye to eye contact and you positively motivate him/her to keep their attention, training can be easy. You will find that your canine will want to work for you when you use a more simplified approach. Your canine will be able to quickly learn wanted behavior, simple commands & be able to more easily avoid distractions when he/she is truly focused on you.

- Focus is a "coping skill". It will allow your canine to relax and trust the handler.
- Eye to Eye contact is your goal. Not an occasional gaze or glance in your direction.
- Once you are able to focus your canine, in many cases, just by calling his/her name will stop unwanted behaviors. Your canine's name and the command to "LOOK" should become synonymous quickly. In other words, every time you call his/her name, your canine is expected to turn their head and look directly at "you".

## 12 Steps to Success

- When your canine is truly focused on you, he/she will become more relaxed, similar to a temporary "wait state of mind" watching and waiting for his/her next command.

- Focus is a basic behavior for humans, however in most cases, focus it is a learned behavior for canines. Focus becomes more important as your training progresses. The more difficult the command, the more focus from your canine it requires. That is why "LOOK "is the first command your canine should learn. It takes time to develop focus skills and connection with your canine, especially when they are young and there are many distractions. Only you can create the focused canine that you desire.

- If your canine has a nervous disposition; <u>focusing on you</u> will be calming to him/her.
- Focus builds trust between you and your canine.

- Focus requires your canine to <u>ignore distractions</u> therefore placing *you* in the alpha-leadership role & providing you with more control over his/her behavior.
- Your canine cannot look at you <u>in a focus state of mind</u>, and bark, lung etc. nor can he or she remain in a "prey state" of mind.

# 12 Steps to Success

- Canines, especially young ones, will be curious about new surrounds & should want to look around to smell and mark their new environment. <u>Allow him/her to experience all the new scents, sounds and people.</u> However, when he/she <u>becomes overly excited,</u> you will need to <u>refocus them immediately.</u> Use your <u>canines name, your body language</u> and <u>scent</u> along with the command "<u>LOOK</u>".

- If you do not regain focus, <u>when excitement begins,</u> it will become <u>more difficult</u> for you <u>to regain control.</u> A canine's ability to listen and focus becomes increasingly difficult once he/she has reached a high state of excitement or a "prey" state of mind.

# "FOCUS WILL REGAIN CONTROL"

- When you have a canine that has a dominate disposition and wants to be in charge, focus on you is the best way to <u>reinforce your leadership & Alpha status.</u>
- The key is catch & correct the excited behavior <u>BEFORE</u> it begins and escalates.
- Upon seeing a distraction that could take your canine's focus away from you or can potentially put them in "prey mode", for example: a squirrel or a rabbit, place <u>yourself in front of your canine,</u> <u>use scent</u> between your fingers, <u>nose tap</u> (when necessary) and refocus him/her quickly by commanding "LOOK". Re-focus your canine quickly as it will help you keep or regain your control over his/her behavior.

## "DONNA & HONEY"

# The Art of Focusing Your Canine

## "LOOK" is the command!

## Only <u>YOU</u> Can Make Your Canine a SHARPLY Focused - Trained Canine

## *"Focus"*

Regardless of what type of training you need or want, <u>FOCUS</u> is the key to all training success. True focus is "eye to eye", contact with you. Whether it is Basic Obedience or Advanced Off-Lead training, Focus is a <u>crucial learned behavior</u>. This one behavior will build a strong, lifelong foundation for you and your canine.

Most puppy & dog training success depends on how well <u>you</u> can focus your canine - - on you. Remember, looking at or towards your face is <u>NOT</u> actually "looking at you". You want your pup to look directly into your eyes. Gazing in your direction does not create focus. Eye to Eye contact is your goal.

"LOOK" is the first command taught in THE One Minute Dog Trainer Program. Focus will assist you with both heel walking and leash manners as both are fully depend on this one complex behavior.

## "ACE – DONNA – ROCKY"

## "Focus"

When a <u>canine is unfocused</u> it is generally the reason he/she does not do well when in a heel walk. When canines are moving forward they are often times ignoring you. They are focusing on the other things going on in the background. Focusing on "you" when something or someone else has got their attention is difficult at best for most canines.

The learned behavior to "<u>LOOK</u>" every time you call your canine's name- can turn things around. It will inevitably make your training easier, quicker and more successful from many perspectives.

Most times, the only eye contact young canine makes with humans a, is momentarily, for instance when your canine is first learning his/her name, you continually call them, they begin to turn their head, look "towards" you. Then usually, they will either run off in a different direction or continue their previous course of action.

## "DONNA & ACE"

# *"Focus"*

Canines will however, look intensely at another dog, cat or squirrel but not so much at humans. Some pups find looking at humans threatening. This is very common. Focused eye contact with a human is not necessarily instinctual, unless a pup is looking to protect something they have or want.

Similarly, if your canine has been through other previous training, yet has not learned to focus on you, it is common for them to run through a gamete of other learned behaviors. You should ignore those behaviors by re-focusing your canine.

Eventually he/she will get it. The true key is <u>your</u> patience & willingness to work with your canine. When you become frustrated, you need to end your training session unless you are willing....wait it out. Frustration is view by a canine as negative energy. Since pups live on Energy, Instinct and Emotion, he/she will pick upon your disapproval. Don't give up! Like a pre-school age child, they need your consistency.

**"Patrick & Donna"**

**"Leading Edge - Hand Commands" are extremely successful. Your body language will GUIDE your canine into the exact behavior you desire.**

# Chapter 14

# *Working Leading Edge Hand Commands*

## Rules to Success

- When first beginning to work (teach) your canine use on lead.
- Use the lead for a minimum of the first 3 to 6 months.
- Use scent to active your canine's mucus membranes in your canine's nose.
- When activating their mucus membranes in a canine's nose, you are enabling his/her brain to move forward which assists your canine in wanting to learn.
- You will be able to do just about every command when scent is placed properly between your first 2 fingers.
- Always begin your sessions with the command "LOOK".
- Repeat "LOOK" before, during and after EVERY command. (Should your canine not be focused on you)
- "NOSE TAP" your canine using the knuckles of the fingers which are holding scent. Tap your canine's nose, use his/her name, this is a subtle correction.
- If your canine is already focusing on you - praise him/her for being focused... "Yes! Good looking", then continue with the next command.
- When first starting out, work commands in SHORT durations. Begin with "ONE" minute.
- When adding more work time, be sure to add time (1) minute at a time,
- ONLY increase duration of your work sessions when you have determined your canine can tolerate additional time. Increase duration slowly.
- DO NOT over work your canine. It will prove counterproductive.
- Adding distance, duration and distraction takes time. Minimum of 3 to 6 weeks of constant practice
- Your canine should be proficient with each command before you can begin to add duration, distance and distraction to that command. (The 3 D's)
- Praise = YES + GOOD + COMMAND

**Why use YES when praising?** - It is important to **verbally agree** with your canine's wanted behavior. In addition, using the word "**YES** "**builds confidence** in your canine.

**Why say GOOD when praising?** The word "**GOOD** "reinforces the wanted behavior/command that you asked for.

**Add the COMMAND when you are praising.** Adding the command to praise teaches & reinforces "THE" wanted behavior you are teaching.

*Command Worksheet*

# "LOOK" - ("at me") or ("right here")

(Eventually you will only command "LOOK")

**Peace sign,** (first **2** fingers) **palm facing you,** wrist _action,_ flexing your wrist **from** your **canine's nose** the to the **bridge** of **your nose**

- Use <u>SCENT</u> (treat) <u>treat between your pointer and middle fingers.</u>
- Waive the treat <u>past your canine's nose</u> as you move your fingers upward toward your eyes. (To the bridge of your nose)
- Use <u>2</u> fingers when pointing from your canine's nose to the bridge of your nose, close to your eyes.
- It will be helpful to make <u>noise with</u> your <u>mouth</u> to keep your canine's attention towards your face for instance a clicking sound.
- "<u>Nose nap</u>" your canine, <u>using the knuckles of your fingers</u> that you are holding the scent with.
- "<u>Nose Tapping</u>" is a <u>subtle correction</u> and will provide additional focus.
- Use your <u>canine's name.</u> This conditions your canine <u>his/her name</u> & the command "<u>LOOK</u>" are <u>one in the same.</u>
- If your canine is <u>looking down, lower your 2 fingers</u> holding scent to your <u>canine's eye level,</u> nose tap him/her and re-command "LOOK".
- If your canine is <u>looking away,</u> you may need to <u>hold their lower jaw</u> to assist in getting their attention.
- In the beginning, you will <u>emphasize the words "AT ME"</u> or "RIGHT <u>HERE"</u> when <u>pointing your 2 fingers in your direction, toward your eyes.</u> (Eventually you will only command "LOOK")
- Be Patient as the "LOOK" command can be intimidating to a young canine who is not naturally comfortable with eye to eye contact.

*Command Worksheet*

## "**LOOK**" Continued

Example: Ellie….Look, Look – (**nose tap**) - at me . . . Using <u>**2 fingers**</u> to point to the bridge of your nose.

## Command "LOOK" - - ("At Me") or ("Right Here")
## Praise: (Upon your canine <u>locking</u> <u>eyes</u> with you)
## YES! YES! Good looking!!!

- Note: If your canine is <u>not focused</u> (looking) at you, <u>repeat the command</u> "LOOK" <u>before, during & after every command</u> use the "nose tapping" method if necessary for additional focus.

*Command Worksheet*

# "TOUCH"

**1 Open hand, <u>Palm facing away</u>** from your canine.

- Scent (treat) <u>between your first 2 fingers.</u>
- Your <u>fingers facing down</u>, towards the ground
- Lightly "<u>Nose Tap</u>" with the <u>outside</u> of <u>your open hand</u>, allowing your canine to smell the scent and <u>touch your hand with his NOSE ONLY.</u> Command "Touch".
- If your canine opens his/her mouth, correct immediately. <u>HEY!</u> & re-command "<u>TOUCH</u>" in <u>a strong assertive voice</u>, as you <u>lightly</u> tap your canine's nose showing your canine that a "<u>Nose Touch ONLY</u>" is all you want.
- When your canine touches your hand <u>without opening his/her mouth</u>, <u>IMMEDIATELY</u> agree with the behavior by saying YES!
- <u>Only release the treat</u> when your canine <u>touches (NOSE ONLY)</u> your hand <u>without opening his/her mouth</u> - on their own.
- Release the treat <u>sporadically.</u> Sine your canine will be unsure when you will release the treat, they are more likely to continue to "<u>TOUCH</u>", NOSE ONLY.

Touch – Allow your canine to touch your hand with his <u>nose ONLY!</u> Yes!
Touch – Allow your canine to touch your hand with his <u>nose ONLY!</u> Yes!
**Touch – Yes! Good Touching (release the treat)**

*Command Worksheet*

# "TOUCH" continued

Start again.  Repeat the command "Touch" as often as possible.
Release the treat **sporadically** & release the treat **after** using the word the word **YES!**

**Touch** – Allow your canine to touch your hand with his <u>nose ONLY</u>! Yes!
**Touch** – Allow your canine to touch your hand with his <u>nose ONLY</u>! Yes!
**Touch** – Allow your canine to touch your hand with his <u>nose ONLY</u>! Yes!
**Touch** – Allow your canine to touch your hand with his <u>nose ONLY</u>! Yes!
**Touch – Yes! Good Touching (release the treat)**

The "**TOUCH**" command will assist you in a few ways.
> 1 – Teaches your canine <u>not to "mouth"</u> you for attention.
> 2 - Shows your canine they <u>can only "touch"</u> you when their <u>mouth is closed</u>
> 3 – When most people greet a dog for the first time, they place the outer part of their hand towards your canine's nose, expecting your canine to smell their hand before they attempt to pet him/her.  The "touch" command will teach your canine to smell (<u>"TOUCH"</u>) when they are greeting.
> 4- When using the command "Touch" <u>as you call your canine towards your hand</u>, you can <u>potentially eliminate</u> some of their <u>excitement and jumping</u> as he/she will be distracted by the "TOUCH" command.

**"DONNA & EINSTEIN"**

**COMMAND = "TOUCH"    PRAISE = YES! GOOD TOUCHING**

*Command Worksheet*

# "SIT"

**(1)** Open Hand, fingers pointing upward, **Palm Facing You,** arm bent at elbow

- Use <u>scent</u> between your <u>first 2 fingers,</u>
- Place 1 open hand, in an upward position, towards your canine's head (close enough to his/her head). Once your canine smells scent they will move their head (back) following scent. Instinctively your canine's hind quarters will move downward into a sit position.
- If your canine is <u>not responding,</u> <u>move your hand closer over his/her head</u> & <u>lean your body in (forward)</u> towards your canine
- Should your pup need additional assistance, <u>place your other hand on his/hers hind quarters</u> and <u>apply light pressure to the hind quarters</u> until he/she is in a <u>full sit</u> (their hind quarters down to the ground).
- Give your canine time to process. <u>Do not be too quick</u> to repeat the command. Remember they are learning. Repeating the command may actually cause your canine to become confused and unfocused.
- Should he/she <u>pop out</u> of the "SIT" command, <u>firmly re-command</u> him/her "SIT", before reward or praise.

**COMMAND = "SIT"    PRAISE = YES! Good Sitting!**

*Command Worksheet*

# "<u>DOWN</u>" ("Lay Down")

**(2) Fingers, <u>Palm Facing Ground,</u>** directly under your canine's nose, place your fingers, using scent, place your fingers **between his/hers front 2 paws. <u>Slowly slide your fingers towards you</u>.** Your pup may "army crawl" but that is okay. **Do not slide your fingers towards you too quickly.** As time goes by, you will be standing upright - pointing 2 fingers toward the ground. I recommended you start from the <u>"SIT"</u> command.

- <u>Scent</u> (treat) between your pointer and middle fingers.
- "Nose tap" your canine with scent - he/she will begin to follow the scent.
- Place your fingers <u>directly under your canine's nose</u>, between his/hers front 2 paws.
- If your fingers are <u>too far away</u>, your canine will pop out of the "SIT" position.
- In general, it is healthier for your canine to go into a "DOWN" from a "SIT" position as it is better for his/her hips as they get older.
- <u>Slowly</u> slide your <u>2 fingers towards you</u>. If you move your fingers too quickly, Canine may stand.
- Your canine will begin to lower his/her head. Immediately begin to agree with the behavior by saying YES!
- To <u>assist</u> your canine, <u>gently hold his/hers lower back</u>, applying <u>minimum pressure</u> to keep him/her <u>firmly in the "SIT"</u> position.
- Only praise or reward when your canine is in a <u>complete "DOWN"</u> position.

**COMMAND = "DOWN"     PRAISE = YES! Good Down**

*Command Worksheet*

# "UP" (From the "DOWN" command)

"**Swing**" **(1) open hand**, over your canine's head, position your hand into a "**Sit position**

(1) Open hand up, **Palm Facing You,** arm bent at elbow.

You will use this command when you want your canine (from a down position) to get ready to move forward. You will also use this command when you want your canine to "hug" you or potentially come up on the sofa if permitted. "On Invite" onto your furniture if you so desire.

- Command "Sit"
- Command "Down"
- Command 'UP" *by* "Swinging" (1) open hand, from the down, directly over your canine's head into a Sit position
- Assist, by using your other hand, placing it under your canine's lower jaw and gently lift him/her into an "UP" (into a "Sit" from "Down").
- Use the lead by placing gentle tension - upward - guiding your canine
- Do not pull strongly on the lead as you do not want your canine to begin coking.

**COMMAND = "UP"**     **PRAISE = "YES" GOOD UP!**

*Command Worksheet*

# "OFF"

**(2) Fingers pointing away from you** or the kitchen counter, or the sofa etc. <u>**Palm Facing Sideways,**</u> a **slight push** with **2 fingers** may be necessary at first. After slightly pushing, point in any direction, away from you, sofa or countertop. Be sure to <u>**divert your canine immediately**</u> after correcting him/her or he/she will soon jump again. Use a toy, bone or ball. Throw the toy, bone or ball <u>**away from you**</u> to <u>**distract your canine from jumping**</u>.

- "LOOK"
- Position yourself <u>in front</u> of your canine should they are on a chair or sofa.
- <u>"Nose tap"</u>
- <u>"LOOK"</u>
- <u>"OFF"</u> Firm commanding voice. <u>Point</u> <u>away</u> from the chair using with <u>2 fingers</u>.
- If necessary, take hold of his/her collar & <u>lead them off of you,</u> sofa etc.
- Depending on your canine's size, as your canine jumps, you can use your knee to defend against the jump. <u>Swing your knee side to side</u>. This will get your canine off balance and force him/her off
- <u>Point away,</u> using <u>2 fingers,</u> firmly correct your canine: OFF! OFF!
- At this point, if you do not <u>immediately redirect</u> your canine, he/she will jump again.
- If your canine is <u>on a lead or tether,</u> <u>tug UP to correct</u> and command <u>"OFF"</u>

When your canine is young, he/she has a limited ability to communicate with you. "Jumping" is instinctual & is one of the ways your canine's is <u>attempting to</u> <u>show you affection</u>. It is exactly how your canine would say hello or play with another canine. Be patient!

**YOUR PUP IS ON THE FURNITURE - - TAKE CONTROL AND COMMAND "OFF"**

# Command Worksheet

# "LEAVE" = Waive 1 (Karate' chop your hand with each waive)

# "IT"= Waive 2 (Karate' chop your hand with each waive)

(2) Separate Waives, Palms facing ground, (over the object). Keep each word & waive separate. Karate' chop your hand with each waive to keep your voice firm. Waiving too quickly can over stimulate your canine.

- "LOOK" -- "AT ME"
- SHOW him/her the object BEFORE placing the object on the floor.
- CLAIM the object using 2 separate Waives. (karate chop your hand)
- Be sure to have to use scent between your first 2 fingers to keep your canine's focus.
- LEAVE = WAIVE # 1 - Karate' chop your hand (Firm commanding voice)
- IT = WAIVE # 2 - Karate' chop your hand (Firm commanding voice)
- Repeat "LOOK" -- "AT ME"
- "Nose tap" using the scent to distract from the object
- Place object on the floor. (Partially cover it with your hand if your canine is overly excited)
- CLAIM the object AGAIN: 2 separate waives. Keep your canine's attention ON YOU & NOT the Object
- Repeat - LEAVE! = WAIVE # 1 Karate' chop your hand
- Repeat - IT! = WAIVE # 2 Karate' chop your hand (Repeat as needed)
- Your canine should NOT be focused or staring at the object. Your goal is your canine IGNORS the object and surrenders. If or when your canine steps back or walks away, that is considered full surrender.
- Repeat NOSE TAP (with scent) to regain your canine's attention if necessary
- Repeat "LOOK" (as needed)
- When he/she begins to focus on you (not the object), quickly agree with his/her behavior. Say "YES!" in a low firm tone of voice.
- Your canine's body language should be in surrender-mode, retreating, or ignoring the object. You want your canine focused on YOU, or surrendering, NOT focused or starring at the object.
- Upon you canine's surrender - Immediately pick up the object.
- DO NOT release your canine to objects while they are on the floor, even if the object is a ball, toy or treat.
- IMMEDIATELY pick up the object and use it with praise.

*Command Worksheet*

# Working "LEAVE - - IT"

This process is called **"Human Claiming"**. Your goal is that your canine **IGNORS** the **object** and remains **focused on you.**

**Photo #1 - Harley's focus is on ME!**    **Photo #2 - Harley is IGNORING the object!**

**COMMAND:**
**LEAVE = WAIVE 1**
**IT! = WAIVE 2**

**PRASIE:**
**YES! Good = WAIVE # 1**
**Leaving It = WAIVE # 2**

Note: IMMEDIATELY pick up the object & use with PRAISE! Waive 2 SEPARATE times (karate' chop your hand) over the object <u>before</u> releasing the object to your canine.

# *Command Worksheet*

## "DROP" = Open Hand Up (You hand appearing as though you are reaching up as if to grab an imaginary handle) Palm Facing Sideways. Firm Commanding voice.

## "IT" = Closed Fist Down (Pull your hand towards you as you close your fist) When imitating a pull down motion towards your body. Palm Facing Sideways

This command applies when your canine **has an object** in his/her mouth that he/she is able to drop. For example: A shoe or sock.

Keep each word & hand positioning - separate. You **do not** want your hand to look as though you are milking a cow (**quick motion**). Moving your hand too quickly can over stimulate your canine.

- Intentionally drop an object to the floor.  For example a sock, paper towel etc.
- Immediately TAKE HOLD of the LEAD.
- Your canine's instinct will be to pick up the object and attempt to run away from you with it.
- You MUST have scent in your hand to ensure your canine will drop at first.
- "Nose Tap" your canine using strong scent for focus. (Repeat "Nose Tap" with scent to entice your canine to drop)
- "LOOK" (Repeat "LOOK" as Needed)
- "Drop" = Open hand up (Scent your canine's nose)
- "It" = Closed fist down (Repeat as Needed)
- Should your canine need assistance, press his/her extra skin of his/her upper snout against his/her teeth. DO NOT press too hard as you want your canine to release on their own.
- Allow him/her time to respond.  Remember they are learning and you want "them" to release if possible.
- If necessary pry your canine's mouth open. And begin again.
- Once he/she releases the object on their own, IMMEDIATELY AGREE with the behavior (YES!) as you pick up the object & use the praise.

## PRAISE USING THE OBJECT
## Object up = "YES! GOOD "   Object down = "DROPPING".

# "DROP - - IT" continued:

- Should your canine **automatically drop** the object, "**praise anyway**"
- **Use the object with praise.** This will condition your canine to the wanted behavior.

IMPORTANT NOTE: <u>DO NOT TUG or PULL!</u> When you <u>tug</u> an object while it is in your canine's mouth as he/she will give you <u>additional resistance</u>, you can <u>unintentionally insight nipping, biting</u> or <u>tug of war</u>.

**COMMAND: "DROP" = Open Hand Up**          **"IT" = Closed Fist Down**

### Praise Using the Object:
### Holding the object up = YES! GOOD
### Bring the object down = DROPPING

<u>DO NOT</u> release your canine to objects on the floor. When you release your canine to objects on the floor, he/she will instinctively assume all objects that fall to the floor "open game". <u>IMMEDIATELY</u> pick up the object and open handedly, <u>PRAISE OVER THE OBJECT</u>. Release the object to your canine from your hand <u>OR</u> reward your canine by engaging in play by throwing the object.

*Command Worksheet*

# "QUIET"    Use this command to control unwanted barking.

We as humans get annoyed when our canines over bark.  However if someone was on your property at 3:00am in the morning, you would want your canine to alert you.  **Expecting a canine not to a bark is like expecting a child not to cry.**  The "__QUIET__" command allows your canine to do what comes naturally, warning you of a disturbance.  **Your response lets your canine know you received the warning bark (alert) and it's ok to stop barking.**

1 raised, open your hand **>-** then lower & close hand slowly >. Use the **Shhhhhh** sound.

Command: QUI = > Open hand - UP
          ET = >  Closed hand DOWN

**COMMAND = "QUI- -ET"**    **PRAISE = YES! Good QUI - - ET**

Keep the word (QUI - - ET) separated on the syllable of the word. Saying the word QUIET as if it were 2 separate words.

# open your hand widely >, then close it slowly ›

NOTE: Fast hand motion (open & closed) resembles the command for "SPEAK"

*Command Worksheet*

# "WAIT"

**(1) Finger pointing UP, <u>Palm facing your canine.</u>** Point into the air, <u>DO NOT point at your canine</u>.

"WAIT" is a "Service Command". You may want to skip this command if your canine reacts well to the Leading Edge Universal Hand command "STAY". "WAIT" can also assist you in teaching your canine patience.

- "LOOK" (Holding scent under your thumb)
- "Nose Tap" If needed for focus
- Command "SIT" – "STAY" or "STAY DOWN"
- Point your (1) finger UP (into the air, not at your canine)
- SLOWLY begin to raise your finger, while at the same time, commanding WAIT - - WAIT - - as you raise your finger.
- SLOWLY begin to lower your finger, while at the same time, commanding WAIT - - WAIT - - as you raise your finger.
- Keep your body still when first beginning to teach this command.
- Wait until your canine to be STILL
- Should your canine begin to fidget, use the SHHHHHHH sound
- Only reward still behavior.

## COMMAND = "WAIT"      PRAISE = YES! Good Waiting!

*Command Worksheet*

# "WAIT" (FROM – TO)

**(1) Finger pointing UP, <u>Palm facing your canine</u>.** Point **towards the sky, <u>DO NOT point at your canine</u>.** After you have worked "WAIT" as a still command, **by not moving your body,** and your canine is remaining still, you can now begin to <u>SLOWLY</u> move away <u>FROM</u> your canine and returning <u>TO</u> your canine.

- "<u>LOOK</u>" - - at me" (Have scent between your fingers.)
- "<u>Nose tap</u>" if necessary for focus.
- Command –"<u>SIT</u>"
- <u>(1) FINGER</u> pointing upward into the air, (not at your canine)
- <u>SLOWLY raise</u> (1) finger as you <u>SLOWLY take a step or two</u> away <u>FROM</u> your canine. <u>Raise finger</u> command WAIT - -STEP BACK - - WAIT - -STEP BACK
- <u>SLOWLY lower</u> (1) finger as you walk <u>BACK TO</u> your canine. <u>LOWER finger</u> command WAIT - -STEP  FORWARD - - WAIT - -STEP FORWARD
- Repeat "<u>LOOK</u>" in a <u>firm assertive voice</u> should your canine begin to look down
- <u>Keep your canine's focus on your hand.</u> If necessary make noise with your mouth or tap the hand holding scent.
- If your canine <u>moves,  re-command (</u>"SIT", take him/her <u>back</u> to the <u>WAIT SPOT</u>
- Start Again.

**COMMAND = "WAIT"    PRAISE = YES!! Good Waiting!**

# "<u>WAIT</u>" (FROM – TO) continued

## COMMAND = "WAIT"
## PRAISE = YES!! Good Waiting!

<u>Important note:</u> The key to being able to move away eventually, from your canine, is to keep your canine's focused on your finger, NOT your feet. Should your canine begins to look down, immediately command "LOOK" which will keep his/her focus on your finger. When your canine looks down, they will instinctively want to follow your feet and begin to move towards you. Stay close until he/she is focused. Be patient! It takes time and practice.

*Command Worksheet*

*Command Worksheet*

# "STAY"

(**1**) Open hand, extended arm, **palm facing your canine.**

- "LOOK "
- "Nose tap" (if necessary for focus).
- Command "SIT" or "DOWN"
- (1) Open hand positioned LOW, just above your canine's nose, have a scent between your fingers.
- Command STAY - - STAY - -STAY in a very firm and assertive voice.
- SLOWLY begin to raise your open hand, continue to command
    STAY - - STAY Keep your body still when first teaching "STAY".
- SLOWLY begin to lower your open hand while repeating the command
    STAY - - STAY Keep your body still when first teaching "STAY".
- Should your canine begin to fidget, use the SHHHHHHH sound from your mouth as most canines find that sound calming.
- Should your canine "pop out" of the "SIT" or "DOWN" re-command, take him/her back to the STAY SPOT where you began.

**COMMAND = "STAY"   PRAISE = YES! GOOD STAYING!!**

*Command Worksheet*

# "<u>STAY</u>" continued

COMMAND = STAY

PRAISE = YES!! Good Staying!

"Shhhhhhh"

*Command Worksheet*

# "**STAY**" Commands:

STAY"= (1) open hand, extended arm, <u>palm facing your canine</u>.

## "<u>SIT</u> <u>STAY</u>"
(SIT) = 1 Open Hand, <u>Palm Facing You,</u> arm bent at elbow
(STAY)= (1) open hand, extended arm, <u>palm facing your canine</u>

## "<u>STAY</u> <u>DOWN</u>"
(DOWN) = 2 fingers, <u>Palm Facing Ground</u>, directly under your canine's nose, between his/hers front 2 paws.
(STAY)= (1) open hand, extended arm, <u>palm facing your canine</u>

## "<u>STAY OFF</u>"

(STAY)= (1) open hand, extended arm, <u>palm facing your canine</u>
(OFF) = 2 **Fingers** pointing away from you, the kitchen counter, or the sofa etc. **Palm facing** <u>sideways.</u> When using "STAY" for the OFF" command, it will be helpful to <u>racket your hand</u> as if you are ready to hit tennis ball, swinging your hand towards your canine, while saying the command "STAY". **This is called "<u>STAY</u>" <u>blocking.</u>**

## "<u>STAY QUIET</u>"
(STAY)= (1) open hand, extended arm, <u>palm facing your canine</u>
(QUIET) = 1 raised open hand (>), lower & close hand. (>) SLOWLY. <u>Palm facing</u> <u>sideways.</u>

*Command Worksheet*

## "STAY" (FROM – TO)

**(1) Open hand,** extended arm, **palm facing your canine.** Occasionally swing your open hand as if you were swinging a tennis racket, palm facing your canine.

- "LOOK"
- "Nose Tap" if necessary for focus.
- Command "SIT"
- Begin with (1) open hand positioned LOW, just above your canine's nose, use scent between your fingers.
- SLOWLY raise hand as you SLOWLY take a step or two AWAY FROM your canine.
- As you are begin to Raise your hand command "STAY" - -STEP BACK - - "STAY" - - STEP BACK
- Once there is a few feet of distance between you and your canine, begin to SLOWLY lower your hand as you walk TO your canine.
- When you begin to LOWER your hand command "STAY" - -SLOWLY STEP FORWARD - - "STAY" - -SLOWLY STEP FORWARD
- Repeat "LOOK" in a firm assertive voice should your canine begin to look down at your feet.
- Keep an eye on your canine's body language STILL, should he/she begin to fidget, use the SHHH sound & continue commanding STAY - - STAY- - while you SLOWLY beginning to walk to your canine.

**COMMAND = "STAY"   PRAISE = YES! Good Staying**

142

*Command Worksheet*

# "COME"

(1) Open extended hand, **palm facing up**, begin waiving toward yourself. Extend your hand out, then move your hand/arm back, waiving alongside of your body, in the direction you want your canine to move.

- Puppies and dogs need to feel welcomed when you call them to come!
- If you are holding onto negative energy when you call your canine to come to you, they will instinctively run in the opposite direction.
- So <u>BE INVITING</u>....
- <u>With an upbeat voice</u>, clap your hands, use your pup's name, "Come" – at <u>FIRST PAW FORWARD</u> begin to <u>agree with the behavior</u>. YES! –YES! "Come"
- By agreeing with his/her movement of their first paw forward this will inspire your canine to continue moving towards you. Should your pup be moving in the opposite direction, <u>call is name</u>, <u>open arms</u>, <u>lean your body forward,</u>
- After time, once your canine knows it is safe to come towards you, you will be able to firmly command, "<u>COME</u>" or "<u>COME</u> <u>HERE</u>" (pointing with 2 fingers to the ground) "<u>RIGHT</u> <u>HERE</u>"

**COMMAND = "COME" PATRICK       PRAISE = YES! YES! GOOD COMING**

*Command Worksheet*

## COMMAND = Harley "COME"    PRAISE = YES! YES! Good Coming!

Important note: No matter what your canine might be doing in the moment you call him/her to "COME", chances are, if you are <u>inviting</u> when calling him/her, they will most likely respond quicker. Using a noise like whistling, clapping, snapping etc. to get his or her attention will <u>also motivate</u> him/her to move towards you.

Should you be <u>upset or angry</u> your <u>canine</u> will sense the <u>negative energy</u> and <u>instinctively retreat</u> away from you. Firm and assertive energies are <u>NOT</u> the same as <u>anger</u> to a pup!

# "STOP" (Into "SIT" – Build a Silent Stay)

(2) Open hands, **palms facing your canine**, extended arms. "**STOP**" command into a "**SIT**" then build a silent "**STAY**"

- "LOOK"
- Begin by standing <u>fairly close</u> to your canine, a few feet away
- Call your canine to come towards you
- Since canines generally run with their heads down, command him/her to "<u>LOOK</u>" if they are looking down or away from you.
- Quickly, however allowing your canine enough time to respond, place 1 foot forward while extending 2 arms forward, hands up, <u>both palms facing your canine</u>.
- Just before your canine arrives to you, command "<u>STOP</u>" Strong assertive voice
- Your canine is expected to <u>stop immediately on command and go into a "SIT"</u>
- In time you will be able to raise your hands and your canine will "<u>STOP</u>" into a "<u>SIT</u>" then build a silent "<u>STAY</u>"

**COMMAND = "STOP"     PRAISE = YES! Good Stopping!**

*Command Worksheet*

# "**Come to STOP**"

Here is how to begin working the "STOP "command. Begin with "**Come to Stop**" as this will teach your canine what the word STOP means. **(His/her Body Stop Moving)**

- Command "<u>SIT</u>"
- Command "<u>STAY</u>"
- Move a few feet away from your canine
- Command "<u>COME</u>"
- <u>Before your canine reaches you</u> – command him or her to "<u>LOOK</u>", if he/she is not looking at you.
- Use <u>His/her NAME</u> - Command "<u>STOP</u>" (2) Open Hands up, extended arms & both palms facing your canine.
  - "<u>STOP</u>" command into a "<u>SIT</u>" then build a silent "<u>STAY</u>"

## "STOP INTO SIT"
## "BISCUIT STOP! YES GOOD STOPPING"

146

*Command Worksheet*

# "<u>STOP</u>" (Along Side)

- After initially practicing & reinforcing the "STOP" command so that your canine is stopping on command.
- Walk with your canine along side of you on lead
- Without notice (You) Stop abroutly, at the same time, use the lead by placing tension slightly upward to guide your canine into a "STOP"
- Command "STOP" - lead up - Into a "SIT" then build a silent "STAY"
- Do not tug as though you are correcting, simply lead you canine by placing tension on the lead.

**Command = STOP  Praise = YES! Good STOPPING**
**(Use the Hand Command in front of your canines eyes to positively reinforce instant stopping)**

# "<u>STOP</u>" from Behind #1 Canines heard things differently from behind, your voice can be muffled so you need to practice **OUTSIDE** where there is little barrier to keep your voice firm.

- Have your canine walk on a <u>6-8 foot lead</u>
- Allow him/her to get <u>ahead of you</u> with the full length of the lead
- Command "STOP" from behind
- Tug up suddenly - creating tension on the lead while commanding "STOP" from behind him/her" - into a "SIT" then build a silent "STAY"
- Upon him/her stopping, use the hand command with praise

## COMMAND = STOP

## PRAISE = YES! Good STOPPING

*Command Worksheet*

# "**STOP**" from Behind #2 (using 2 people and adding distance)

You should teach your canine **all** **commands** **from** **behind** as the command may sound different to your canine when they are not looking at you and/or there is distance between you. For example, when outside there are many <u>distractions</u> and little barriers to keep your voice firm & contained. Although your canine has enhanced hearing, <u>your voice will sound muffled</u> when you are commanding from behind outside. Practice the following to be sure your canine will stop when there is distance and distraction.

- **Person #1** Distract you canine from person #2 – Command "**LOOK**"
- **Create distance** between the 2 humans **20 to 30 feet** is recommended
- **Person # 2** Release your canine by calling him/her to "**COME**"
- Having a ball or toy will be helpful
- **Person # 1 FROM behind** your canine, firmly command "**STOP**"
- **Person #2 NO VERBAL COMMAND**   Person #2 will be **using the hand Command ONLY.** This will showing your canine **with your body** the desired "**STOP**" command into a "**SIT**" then build a silent "**STAY**"

## COMMAND = STOP  PRAISE = YES! Good STOPPING

*Command Worksheet*

# "PLACE"

"**PLACE**" will elevate stress for both you and your canine. Once **you have taught** your canine what "**PLACE**" is and **the expectation of what to do** once he/she get there, you can use "PLACE" for the following reasons.

- The command "PLACE" is **confinement without creating.** Use this command when you want your canine to relax in "**PLACE**" without leaving unless commanded "**FREE**"
- Use this command when the **doorbell rings** to elevate **unwanted excitement, jumping etc.** Use this command when you are **giving your canine a messy bone** or treat and you want the **mess to be confined to one area**.

## Phase I

- Choose an object you wish to eventually call "PLACE".
- You will want to use an "OBJECT" for "PLACE" that will **NOT MOVE** when you're canine walks onto it. (not recommended to use a towel or blanket)
- Choose an object that is <u>slightly raised above the floor or an object that has a different texture the carpet or floor</u> you are working on.
- Have <u>scent</u> in your hand to <u>lure your canine onto the object</u>
- Using a lead, <u>guide your canine</u> to the "<u>object</u> "however <u>DO NOT</u> say the command "PLACE" yet. (You will command "PLACE" once your canine is comfortable stepping onto the object and sitting on it.)
- Use <u>scent</u> in your hand <u>waive towards the object while lowering your hand</u>
- Once your canine is <u>on</u> (all 4 paws) the "OBJECT" - Agree with the behavior "YES" (you should be <u>standing in front</u> of your canine)
- Use the lead and guide your canine <u>away</u> from the "OBJECT"

<u>YES</u>! AGREE WITH THE BEHAVIOR WHEN YOUR CANINE STEPS ONTO "PLACE"

149

*Command Worksheet*

## "PLACE" Phase I CONTINUED

- <u>DO</u> <u>NOT</u> COMMAND <u>STAY</u> –to leave the object you will command "<u>FREE</u>"
- FREE = <u>A waive of your hand</u> away from the object
- Command "<u>FREE</u>" as you <u>walk away</u> from the object guiding your canine (on lead) <u>waving in the direction</u> you are walking.
- Repeat steps above until your canine is comfortable stepping onto and sitting on the object.

## "PLACE" Phase II

- Once you have practiced Phase I, and your canine is <u>comfortable stepping onto</u> the "<u>OBJECT</u>" it is time to begin <u>name the "OBJECT"</u> - "<u>PLACE</u>"
- Practice phase I except now you will be <u>naming</u> the "OBJECT - "<u>PLACE</u>"
- Make sure your your canine is <u>comfortable going to "PLACE"</u> (Into a "<u>SIT</u> & "<u>DOWN</u>") While you are working with your canine in Phase I , <u>stand in front of your canine</u>
- <u>Extend the time</u> you are standing in front of your canine <u>BEFORE releasing the treat</u>
- <u>Using ONE minute as a guideline,</u> continue to extend the time as your canine can tolerate
- <u>SLOWLY</u> walk <u>away</u> creating a nonverbal "STAY"

## Command Worksheet

## "PLACE" Phase III

- You will want to <u>build</u> a "<u>SILENT STAY</u>"
- <u>DO NOT COMMAND</u> "<u>FREE</u>" until you get a <u>few feet away</u> from "<u>PLACE</u>"
- You may need to <u>secure a short lead</u> near "PLACE" to keep your canine in place
- <u>IMMEDIATELY</u> agree with the behavior! <u>YES!</u>
- Once your canine is remaining on "<u>PLACE</u>" until commanded "<u>FREE</u>" begin to extend the <u>distance</u> WITHOUT SAYING THE WORD "FREE"
- Then begin to add duration & distractions <u>BEFORE</u> commanding "<u>FREE</u>"
- Be patient! This command take time and <u>YOUR</u> commitment. If you <u>work this command DAILY,</u> multiple times a day, your canine should <u>be staying on "PLACE" until you command "FREE" in roughly 3 to 4 weeks.</u>

## COMMAND = LEO "PLACE"     MAX - "FREE" TO RELEASE

# How You Greet Your Canine

How <u>you</u> greet your canine is <u>EXACTLY</u> how your canine will greet <u>everyone</u>. Keeping that in mind when you are greeting your canine, you should encourage him/her to greet calmly.  Or the alternative is to <u>use the commands</u> and <u>invite your canine</u> to engage in <u>your greeting.</u> I.E. If your canine is barreling towards you – <u>they will instinctively jump,</u> so you mind as well make the jump ("**UP**") <u>YOUR</u> command.

**COMMAND = "UP"**          **COMMAND ="OFF"**

- Command <u>"UP"</u> BEFORE he/she jumps on you.
- Now you are conditioning him/her that <u>"UP"</u> is a <u>COMMAND</u> not a given.
- If <u>YOU</u> command <u>"UP"</u> & your children command <u>"UP"</u> however your company <u>DOES NOT</u> command ´UP´, your canine will learn that <u>"UP"</u> is <u>on invite.</u>
- Once you have hugged your canine <u>COMMAND</u> – <u>"OFF!"</u> Pointing with 2 fingers away from you and/or your children
- A <u>slight push</u> will most likely be needed to get your canine off of you.
- <u>Distract immediately,</u> try using a squeaking a toy and throwing it away from you.
- All canines want to say hello, <u>so inviting them to excitement and giving affection</u> may calm them down quicker.

# THE HEEL WALK

## Don't walk me, I'll walk you

# "About The Heel Walk"

The command "<u>HEEL</u>" implies, follow me, <u>do not pass my forward heel.</u> Hence the word "<u>HEEL</u>". In other words, I walk you (my loving canine), you won't walk me. Most "<u>humans</u>" become <u>extremely excited</u> before and while getting ready to walk their canines. "<u>Humans</u>" begin the excitement early on in the process by using "<u>lots of high pitched words</u>" and an "<u>extremely upbeat energy</u>" hence, before we get close to the lead and collar, no less attempting putting it on our canine, we literally are coaching our canines to be more and more excited. Sound familiar?

Then of course we humans put the lead and collar on our canines while we continue to "<u>psych out</u>" our canine with <u>more conversation</u>. We say things like: "Come on Buddy!!!!", "Let's go!", "We are going...going outside!", "Are you ready?" At this point the canine is so <u>overly excited</u>, they can hardly contain themselves.

What comes next? Humans open the front door and allow our canine fly out the door ahead of us, yet our canine is now in such an <u>overly stimulated frame of mind</u>, they are pulling your arm out of the socket to get .....OUTSIDE. We all do it or should I say, have done it! <u>We are somehow conditioned to excite our canine to go outside with us</u>. Of course "OUR" expectation, for these very simple minded, instinctual beings...is that "they will just know" how to calm down once we get exit our home, right? Nope.....<u>WRONG!</u>

<u>Your canine needs to learn how to be a follower</u>. It makes an unspoken statement to your canine when you exit your home first. The statement is "this is my walk". Canines need <u>to be taught</u> how to walk along side of you NOT in front (leading) of you. In most cases walking calmly is <u>not a natural instinct</u> for the canine species, especially for young canines. They are curious and want to get out to see the world that exists outside your home. So it is "<u>YOUR</u>" job to <u>condition your canine</u> to your expectations...

## Command Worksheet

# "Heel"

### Step I - Leash On - Wait for Calm:

- Place the lead and collar on your canine in another room, <u>AWAY</u> from the door.
- <u>Start with commands:</u> "LOOK", of course, praise him/her when your canine is following command. Getting your canine into <u>"command/working mode"</u> before you exit your house is a good idea.
- If your canine was conditioned to excitement when going for a walk in the past, it could take time to recondition them. <u>Be patient.</u>
- You need to condition your canine to <u>"your desired behavior"</u> before you get to the front door or exit the house.
- Most trainers are initially taught to "heel walk" a canine on their left side. This is because "most" canines are <u>"right pawed"</u>. Similar to "a higher percentage" of people" being right handed.
- Your canine will "most likely" start with their "right paw" when they begin to walk, therefore you will <u>start with your left foot.</u> For is the reason, I highly suggest you start the heel walk with your canine on your left side, so your canine has a better chance of getting into <u>"your stride'</u> easier.
- Your canine should <u>always be on the curb side</u> (the side closet to the curb) for safety purposes.

**"DONNA & MAX"**

# Command Worksheet

## "HEEL"

## Step II

- Place his/her <u>collar up high</u> (near the ears). The idea is that you want to <u>control</u> your canine's <u>head,</u> like a horse, and <u>not</u> his/her <u>neck or throat</u>
- The <u>lead</u> needs to be <u>short</u>, a foot or two at most, when you are first teaching your canine to heel.
- Practice on your property before heading into the street to ensure you have the focus and control you desire.

## "DONNA & LAYLA"

## Command Worksheet

**"HEEL"**
**Step IV**

- <u>Do not wrap</u> the lead tightly around my hand as it can block your "energy flow" from flowing down lead easily to the canine. More importantly, if you cannot release the lead quickly, should you need to, you could very well get pulled to the ground if you are walking a strong breed such as a German Shepard or Rottweiler.
- Your <u>left arm</u> should be <u>somewhat relaxed</u> when permitted.
- Once outside, <u>start with simple commands.</u> "Look", using a new scent can be helpful. Focus your canine <u>BEFORE</u> distraction come into play.
- Getting your canine to <u>focus</u> <u>before</u> you exit your property <u>is crucial</u>, once distractions are in play it will be more difficult to control your canines' behavior & excitement.

# Command Worksheet

## "Heel"

## Step V

- Before beginning to walk release your pet with any of the following words: "OK", "Ready" or "Come". This should make your canine look in your direction before you start to move.  If not use scent in front of his/nose and command "<u>LOOK</u>"
- Repeatedly commanding "<u>LOOK</u>", will <u>focus your canine</u> and <u>slow him/her down</u>.
- While <u>in motion</u> "LOOK" is a slight <u>tilt their head</u> which represents an acknowledgment of "you".
- You to keep your canine somewhat <u>focused on you</u>.  This will help you see distractions and focus you canine <u>BEFORE</u> distractions get to them.
- Repeat the command "<u>LOOK</u>" as often as needed or if your canine is tilting their head in your direction from time to time, <u>praise them</u> for "LOOKING" <u>while in motion</u>.
- If/when your canine begins to pull correct him/her by <u>tugging up</u> on the lead Command <u>HEEL!</u>
- Continue to walk at a decent pace but do not allow your canine to set the pace.
- When your canine is pulling <u>(YOU) need to STOP</u> and <u>correct</u> by using an assertive tug on the lead. Your correction should be assertive, tug either <u>straight up</u> or <u>towards you</u>.
- <u>DO NOT tug in a backward motion</u> as when you tug back, you are encouraging your canine to pull forward.  It is an instinct for a canine to pull forward when being tugged back.
- <u>Auto Sit When You Stop</u> – Scuffing your feet just before you are ready to stop is drawing your canine's attention to your feet.  Potentially slowing him/her down.
- Upon stopping <u>wait</u> to see if your canine will automatically sit (non-verbal).  Try your best to <u>NOT SAY "SIT"</u>. If your canine doesn't sit, command "LOOK!"
- If necessary, <u>place your left foot</u> (your foot closet to your pet) <u>back</u> toward the rear of your canine <u>while holding tension on the lead</u>.  Use the lead to guide him/her into a sit.
- Give them time to respond. Canines need time to process. Sitting when you stop can be an auto-NON VERBAL response if you wait it out.

# Command Worksheet

**"HEEL"**
**Step VI**
**PRAISE them OFTEN when they look, sit etc. to reinforce wanted behavior.** YES! Good sitting

- If your lead is short, as it should be when heeling, your canine should be fairly <u>lined up</u> (aligned) with you (the same direction your body is facing)
- If your canine <u>is not aligned</u> with you, <u>align your body to your canine</u>. Your goal is to condition your canine to be facing in the same direction as you every time you stop. In time, by aligning your body to your canine's position, your canine will automatically begin to align their body with you when you stop movement.
- Stop and start often. HAVE FUN!!!!!!!! Don't get too serious. Keep it light and make it easy.
- Upon entering your home, <u>you should be the first one inside</u>, even if only by a step. Your home, Your Walk!
- When you do not interact with your canine on a walk, it is "their" walk. Most canines are not ready for silence during the walk for 3 to 6 months, depending upon how much you practice.
- Start off with <u>short periods of time</u>.
- Practice for <u>5 or 10 minutes</u> a few times a day when possible.
- Your desire is loose lead walking & focus!

**"MY FRIEND IRINA & HER AWARD WINNING GERMAN SHEPERD QUANT"**

# Chapter 15

# *Tug-of-War & Your Canine*

## THE dog trainer's opinion

**Question:** Can Tug-of-War make my canine aggressive?

**Answer:** No. Tug-of-War is a tremendous predatory energy burner, good exercise for your canine and will even help your canine through their aching teething periods. When played with the proper rules.

**The game <u>doesn't</u> make your canine a predator – Canines are born predators!**

# Why Canine Parents are Steered Away from the Game

Canine owners have been steered away from Tug-of-War because of the many misnomers of the risk of it increasing aggression and/or dominance in the canine. Many canine resource people such as breeders, trainers and veterinarians caution against this game. This is partly a failure to discriminate between <u>agonistic behavior</u> (conflict resolution & defensive aggression) and <u>predatory behavior</u>.

Many humans have issues about witnessing intensity of the "Play". **<u>Intensity is not aggression</u>**!

**Played with rules:** Tug-of-War can serve as a barometer of the kind of control <u>you have</u> over your canine, more importantly <u>over his/her jaws</u>. It can be fun & safe when you know the game and teach the rules.

# Tug of War

# Know the Game so You Can Teach the Game!

Young canines, much like infants, have extra fluid in their brain until they are fully grown. Full growth can take up to 12 to 15 months, depending upon the breed of Canine. If the game is allowed to be played too aggressively by a human, it can leave significant, negative long term effects on a canine's brain, not only physically but mentally.

What you teach you canine is what you get! You can be unknowingly be teaching your canine dominance and aggression. It is up to you, the human, to know & teach the rules before you play the game. Furthermore it is up to you to teach your family & children the rules so that your canine does not become confused. Children, especially young children need to know the <u>dos and don'ts</u> of the game.

Tug-of-War can have many positive outcomes when <u>taught</u> to your canine safely and correctly with rules. The game can serve as an outlet. It's intense, <u>increases your canine's focus and confidence.</u> The big payoff is in lowered incidence of behavior problems due to under stimulation and a potent motivator for snappy obedience.

<u>Control the games, control the dog</u>. It's also extremely efficient in terms of space and time requirements. If tug of war is correctly installed (taught & played), when you're playing and your canine "wins," i.e. you let go, he will try to get you to re-engage in the game rather than leaving and hoarding.

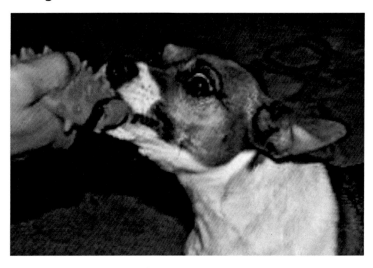

# Tug of War Rules: You must teach your Canine the rules

- <u>Specific initiation command</u>
- Teach your canine the command "Take". On Command ONLY
- <u>Specific release command:</u>
- <u>Choose your word!</u> "Out", ""Drop It", "Release"
- Make sure your family knows the command and is consistent with it. "Out"-on-command is motivated initially with food rewards and later maintained with re-initiation of the game when the dog outs and a time-penalty or game-misconduct for failures to "out".
- Teach you canine "Out", "Drop It" or "Release" On Command <u>ALWAYS</u>
- Designated Object: The Tug of War game is only played with <u>ONE specific object</u> and never with anything else until your canine is older OR has <u>full knowledge</u> of the game.
- <u>No Uninvited Takes or Re-Takes:</u>
- Your canine <u>must not grab</u> the object before the initiation "Take" command or else he/she faces a time-penalty or game-misconduct (the game stops)
- <u>Frequent "Obedience Breaks" in the Action:</u>
- These are "outs" followed by a bit of obedience training (sit-down-tricks) followed by re-initiation of the game with a ("Take" command) as reward
- <u>Jaw Prudence:</u> Your canine should <u>never nick your skin</u> or he faces a game-misconduct (Time out from the game). Even if you deliberately "feed" a canine your hand, he <u>must go</u> <u>out of his way to avoid it.</u> <u>No exceptions</u>

If tug of war <u>has not been correctly</u> taught & played, your canine will leave and hoard when he wins. Don't panic about whose dominant when this happens, simply avoid key tactical errors.

- Play hard to get - rather than chasing your canine.
- Show zero interest or investment in the object.
- Avoid battles with your canine involving speed and agility - you cannot win. Psych-outs are much better.
- Pretend you couldn't care less or even notice. Then reward steps in the right direction. Be patient.
- The goal is for your canine to learn that the object is infinitely more fun when brought to life <u>by you</u> than when it is dead.(not being touched by a human)

# Chapter 16

# *Service Animal Program*

# THE dog trainer LI, Inc.

THE dog trainer LI, Inc. Service Animal Program provides you the opportunity to learn how to train your own Service Dog with guidance from an experienced Master Canine Trainer. In this chapter you will find the **Federal Government Guidelines** that you are expected to be aware of when deciding to train your own Service Animal.

Service Animal Summary

House Manners:
        Why does it matter if you dog is well behaved at home? Because good (or bad) dog behavior spills over into all aspects of a dog's training. If a canine is overly excited & jumping when greeting guests, becomes crazy when the mail man shows up, it will be more difficult to get good manners from him/her in public. Your Service Animal <u>does not</u> get to choose who he/she likes or do not like. Greeting in public is one of the most important aspects of a Service Animal Training.

Lifestyle Training
        It is important to work commands with your canine where you live, work and play. If your Service Animal will eventually go with you to watch the kids' soccer games or go to the bus stop to greet the children, go to work with you or accompany your college-aged son or daughter to school – you will need to train your canine in those places. If you're like me and eat out a lot, you will need to work your canine at restaurants to make sure your canine does not react when the waiter/waitress comes to your table.   Does not react when food is brought to your table and for sure DOES NOT beg while in public. Your Service Animal must fit into "your" lifestyle and know how to respond or not, when servicing you.

What are the challenges of training your own service animal?
        It can be a lot of work and so if you've never had a dog or never "trained" a dog, it can be challenging. Service Animal training can be time consuming, there are times when it could take up to a year. Since all canines are not the same, training a canine never ups and downs, however if you don't give up, it will be worth your efforts in the end.  You need follows one straight line from beginning to end, it can get frustrating at times. You will have to be determined and willing to put the time in, so you can have the Service Animal you desire.   It is ultimately YOUR commitment to yourself & your canine that will get you through the Service Requirement Program.

## Service Animal Summary

What are the rewards of training your own service animal?

First, the bond that is created by spending hours (at first, in small increments of time) working with your canine is very powerful. If you were to have a trained adult service dog magically delivered to your door that relationship would be entirely different from the one you will have with a Service Animal you have trained yourself.

There is a therapeutic value of training your own Service Animal. Perhaps that alone is one of the best benefits. If you suffer from depression, anxiety or a fear of being around people in public ... as you train your canine, he/she will come to understand you better and they will learn, in time, what you need from them. The right dog will help you through the rough times, getting you outside yourself and <u>focused</u> on him/her - that joyous, wagging, silly, loving ball of fur who will become your best friend. The pride that you will feel as you train your Service Animal to do more and more challenging things will build your self-esteem, culminating in a lifelong partnership based on mutual respect.

## Dog Breeds

The US Department of Justice does not require a specific breed of canine for service training. I have worked with many different breeds of canines such as: Labrador Retrievers, German Shepherds, Golden Retrievers, Australian Shepherds, Golden-Doodles, Morkies, Maltese, Maltipoos, Bichons, Teddy Bears and many, many others.

More important than breed of a canine is his/her <u>temperament</u> and <u>trainability</u>. It is important you understand "more" is expected from a Service Animal. There are Federal Guidelines designed to protect not only you & your Service Animal, but they also to protect business owners and the surrounding public.  Think about it this way: what would you expect from a Service Animal if you were eating dinner with a friend? Excitement?  Barking? Begging? As a Service Animal Owner you must be in control (using 1 & 2 word commands) at all times, both on leash and if applicable - off Leash.

# Handler Information for

# Service Animals

**"PATRICK IS ONE OF THE BEST PROFESSIONALLY TRAINED SERVICE ANIMALS"**

# Service Handler Information

Below you will find some of the most frequently-asked questions about service dogs.

## Is there any application to fill out?

There are no applications to fill out and you do not need a doctor's note. Your service animal must be registered with a legitimate registry. The American Animal Academy uses the United States Dog Registry. It is a onetime registration that never requires renewal.

## Can I have a service dog?

If you have a disability (a physical or mental impairment that substantially limits one or more major life activities of such individual) then you are entitled to a service animal to do work or perform tasks for you. You are never required to disclose what your disability is to anyone, nor is anyone allowed to ask about your disability, require medical documentation, require a special identification card or training documentation for the service animal, or ask you or your canine to demonstrate your canine's ability to perform the work or task.

## What breed of dog can be considered a service animal?

Under ADA law any breed of dog can be considered a service animal.

## Do I have to pay any extra fees?

No - No businesses, apartments or airlines can charge you extra fees in order to have your service dog by your side.

## Is PTSD covered?

Yes, PTSD (Post-Traumatic Stress Disorder) is covered under ADA Laws and as long as your service animal is able to calm you during an anxiety attack then he/she is considered a service animal.

## Can I take my dog anywhere?

Once your canine is considered a service animal you can take them with you anywhere the public has access to as long as they are not misbehaving.

My landlord says, "NO PETS ALLOWED"; can I have my emotional support dog with me?

Once your dog is trained, he/she is considered a service animal, he or she can stay with you at your residence even if there are no allow pets.

## Service Handler Information

### Service Animal Training Requirements

- Your canine should know all basic commands, on and off leash.
- Your canine is required to be able to greet people without barking and jumping, unless invited to do so.
- You should be able to command your canine to come when called, sit, down, stay, stop, heel etc.
- You should have full control over your canine's barking while in public, regardless of the situation.
- It is suggested that both you and your pet display Photo ID when in public, identifying you as your pet's handler, your pet's photo & Service Pet Federal Law.
- A Service Pet Vest is suggested, however may not be required in all states. Check with your local township for additional information.
- It is highly suggested to consult with a professional trainer. If you are using a professional trainer, the company information should be properly displayed on your pet's photo I.D.

What if someone has a fear or allergy of dogs, will my service dog be allowed?

Allergies and fear of dogs are not valid reasons for denying access or refusing service to people using service dogs. When a person who is allergic to canine dander and a person who uses a service animal must spend time in the same room or facility, for example, in a school classroom or at a homeless shelter, they both should be accommodated by assigning them, if possible, to different locations within the room or different rooms in the facility.

Can I be asked to leave if my service dog is being disruptive?

Yes. A person with a disability cannot be asked to remove his service animal from the premises unless:

(1) The service animal is out of control and the handler does not take effective action to control it

(2) The dog is not housebroken. When there is a legitimate reason to ask that a service dog be removed, staff must offer the person with the disability the opportunity to obtain goods or services without the animal's presence.

## Service Handler Information

Does my service dog have to be on a leash?

Under the ADA, <u>service animals must be harnessed, leashed, or tethered,</u> unless these devices interfere with the service dog's work or the individual's disability prevents using these devices. In that case, the individual must maintain control of the animal through voice, signal, or other effective controls.

What do I do if I am refused entry or questioned by a business?

There are <u>only two questions</u> you may be asked regarding your service animal:

1) Is the canine a service animal required <u>because</u> of a disability?

2) What work or task has the animal been trained to perform. (NO DEMONSTRATION REQUIRED)

Staff <u>cannot ask about</u> the <u>person's disability,</u> require medical documentation, require a special identification card or training documentation for the canine, or ask that your canine demonstrate its ability to perform the work or task.

Are businesses allowed to question me or refuse to give me service?

No. <u>Under the ADA, you are allowed to take your service animal virtually anywhere you are allowed to go. Your canine, once trained, is not considered a "pet".</u> You are allowed to have your service animal with you in your apartment, restaurants, beaches, airplanes, etc., all without having to pay any extra fees or deposits.

What information is shown on the ID card?
The information provided on a service animal ID is:
(1) Service Animal's, <u>Name</u> and (2) <u>registration number</u>

2 - Optional picture (ID card only), and service animal <u>Name</u> and <u>registration number.</u> If you are using a professional trainer, the company name should appear on your service dog's I.D. Card.

What's the purpose of the certificate and the ID card?

The purpose of the ID kit and vest is so <u>others are aware of the fact that the canine is a service animal.</u> It is to drive awareness to those around you since people often have a difficult time without the vest and ID. An ID & vest will also assist you in not having your service animal constantly interrupted by the public wanting to handle (say hello or pet) him/her

Some businesses, <u>such as airlines,</u> will ask that the canine be wearing a clearly-marked vest or have some form of identification card for the canine.

# Service Animals
# &
# Business Owners

## Business Owners

o   What are the laws that apply to my business?

Under the Americans with Disabilities Act (ADA), privately owned businesses that serve the public, such as restaurants, hotels, retail stores, taxicabs, theaters, concert halls, and sports facilities, are prohibited from discriminating against individuals with disabilities. The ADA requires these businesses to allow people with disabilities to bring their service animals onto business premises in whatever areas customers are generally allowed.

What is a service animal?
The ADA defines a service animal as <u>any</u> guide dog, signal dog, or other animal individually trained to provide assistance to an individual with a disability. If they meet this definition, animals are considered service animals under the ADA regardless of whether they have been licensed or certified by a state or local government.

• Service animals perform some of the functions and tasks that the individual with a disability cannot perform for him or herself. Guide dogs are one type of service animal, used by some individuals who are blind. This is the type of service animal with which most people are familiar. But there are service animals that assist persons with other kinds of disabilities in their day-to-day activities. Some examples include:

1. Alerting persons with hearing impairments to sounds.
2. Pulling wheelchairs or carrying and picking up things for persons with mobility impairments.
3. Assisting persons with mobility impairments with balance.
4. A service animal is <u>not</u> considered a pet.

"YOU CAN TAKE YOUR SERVICE ANIMALS ANYWHERE, WHEN THEY ARE TRAINED PROPERLY"

## Business Owners

- How can I tell if an animal is really a service animal and not just a pet?

Some, but not all, service animals wear special collars and harnesses. Some, but not all, are licensed or certified and have identification papers. If you are not certain that an animal is a service animal, you may ask the person who has the animal if it is a service animal required because of a disability. However, an individual who is going to a restaurant or theater is not likely to be carrying documentation of his or her medical condition or disability. Therefore, such documentation generally may not be required as a condition for providing service to an individual accompanied by a service animal. Although a number of states have programs to certify service animals, you may not insist on proof of state certification before permitting the service animal to accompany the person with a disability.

- What must I do when an individual with a service animal comes to my business?

Service animal must be permitted to accompany the individual with a disability to all areas of the facility where customers are normally allowed to go. An individual with a service animal may not be segregated from other customers.

- I have always had a clearly posted "no pets" policy at my establishment. Do I still have to allow service animals in?

Yes. A service animal is <u>not</u> a pet. The ADA requires you to modify your "no pets" policy to allow the use of a service animal by a person with a disability. This does not mean you must abandon your "no pets" policy altogether but simply that you must make an exception to your general rule for service animals.

- My county health department has told me that <u>only</u> a guide dog has to be admitted. If I follow those regulations, am I violating the ADA?

Yes, if you refuse to admit any other type of service animal on the basis of local health department regulations or other state or local laws. <u>The ADA provides greater protection for individuals with disabilities and so it takes priority over the local or state laws or regulations.</u>

## Business Owners

- Can I charge a maintenance or cleaning fee for customers who bring service animals into my business?

No. Neither a deposit nor a surcharge may be imposed on an individual with a disability as a condition to allowing a service animal to accompany the individual with a disability, even if deposits are routinely required for pets. However, a public accommodation may charge its customers with disabilities if a service animal causes damage so long as it is the regular practice of the entity to charge non-disabled customers for the same types of damages. For example, a hotel can charge a guest with a disability for the cost of repairing or cleaning furniture damaged by a service animal if it is the hotel's policy to charge when non-disabled guests cause such damage.

- I operate a private taxicab and I don't want animals in my taxi; they smell, shed hair and sometimes have "accidents." Am I violating the ADA if I refuse to pick up someone with a service animal?

Yes. Taxicab companies may not refuse to provide services to individuals with disabilities. Private taxicab companies are also prohibited from charging higher fares or fees for transporting individuals with disabilities and their service animals than they charge to other persons for the same or equivalent service.

- Am I responsible for the animal while the person with a disability is in my business?

No. The care or supervision of a service animal is solely the responsibility of his or her owner. You are not required to provide care or food or a special location for the animal.

- What if a service animal barks or growls at other people, or otherwise acts out of control?

You may exclude any animal, including a service animal, from your facility when that animal's behavior poses a direct threat to the health or safety of others. For example, any service animal that displays vicious behavior towards other guests or customers may be excluded. You may not make assumptions, however, about how a particular animal is likely to behave based on your past experience with other animals. Each situation must be considered individually.

## Business Owners

- What if a service animal barks or growls at other people, or otherwise acts out of control?

  Although a public accommodation may exclude any service animal that is out of control, it should give the individual with a disability who uses the service animal the option of continuing to enjoy its goods and services without having the service animal on the premises.

- Can I exclude an animal that doesn't really seem dangerous but is disruptive to my business?

  There may be a few circumstances when a public accommodation is not required to accommodate a service animal–that is, when doing so would result in a fundamental alteration to the nature of the business. Generally, this is not likely to occur in restaurants, hotels, retail stores, theaters, concert halls, and sports facilities. But when it does, for example, when a dog barks during a movie, the animal can be excluded.

**Should you have further questions about service animals or other requirements of the ADA, you may call the U.S. Department of Justice's toll-free ADA Information Line at 800-514-0301 (voice) or 800-514-0383 (TDD)**

# US Department of Justice
## Service Dog Requirements

**Information provided by:**

**U.S. Department of Justice
Civil Rights Division**

**Service Animal Requirements**

The U.S. Department of Justice Civil Rights Division does provide actual requirements in regards to Service Dog. The requirements serve as a "guideline"

For Service Dog Registration. U.S. Department of Justice has put in place an "Honor System". Meaning although <u>there are specific requirements issued by the U.S. Department of Justice to qualify pets to become Service Animals, for the most part, persons can register their pet under the assumption the requirements have been met.</u> Unfortunately, in most cases, only those persons desiring their canine to actually provide a "service" to them, follow through with the filed requirements. Below please find the requirements set forth by the US Department of Justice.

# Service Animal Training Requirements

1. <u>Amount of Schooling</u>: an assistance dog should be given a minimum of one hundred twenty <u>(120) hours of schooling over a period of Six Months or more</u>.* At least thirty <u>(30) hours should be devoted to outings</u> that will prepare the canine to <u>work obediently and unobtrusively in public places.</u>

2. <u>Obedience Training</u>: a canine must master the basic obedience skills: "Sit, Stay, Come, Down, Heel" and a dropped leash recall in a store in <u>response to verbal commands and/or hand signals.</u>

3. <u>Manners</u>: a dog must acquire proper social behavior skills. It includes at a minimum:

- No aggressive behavior toward people or other animals - no biting, snapping, snarling, growling or lunging and barking at them when working off your property.
- No soliciting food or petting from other people while on duty.
- No sniffing merchandise or people or intruding into another dog's space while on duty.
- Socialize to tolerate strange sights, sounds, odors etc. in a wide variety of public settings.
- Ignores food on the floor or dropped in the canines' vicinity while working outside the home.
- Works calmly on leash. No unruly behavior or unnecessary vocalizations in public settings. No urinating or defecating in public unless given a specific command or signal to toilet in an appropriate place.

## Service Animal Requirements

4. Disability Related Tasks: the dog must be individually trained to perform identifiable tasks on command or cue for the benefit of the disabled human partner. This includes alerting to sounds, medical problems, certain scents like peanuts or situations if training is involved.

5. Prohibited Training: Any training that arouses a dog's prey drive or fear to elicit a display of aggression for guard or defense purposes is strictly prohibited. Non aggressive barking as a trained behavior is permitted in appropriate situations.

6. A Trainer's Responsibilities: Trainers function as ambassadors for the assistance dog movement. This includes a disabled owner, professional trainer, a provider's staff or a volunteer with a puppy or adult dog "in training." It also includes an assistance dog partner or able bodied facilitator helping a disabled loved one to keep up an assistance dog's training. At a minimum, you should:

- Know pertinent canine laws (i.e. leash laws and public access laws)
- Ensure the canine is healthy, flea free and the rabies vaccination is up to date
- Take time to make sure your dog is well groomed and free of any foul odor
- Show respect and consideration to other people and property.
- Use humane training methods; monitor the canine's stress level; provide rest breaks.
- Carry clean up materials. Arrange for prompt clean up if a canine eliminates or gets sick.
- Be polite and willing to educate the public about assistance dogs and access rights.

**The 120 hours of schooling includes the time invested in home training sessions, obedience classes or lessons from an experienced canine trainer.**

# Public Access Test Requirements:

The Public Access Test evaluates the dog's obedience and manners and the handler's skills in a variety of situations which include:

A. The handler's abilities to:

( 1 ) safely load and unload the dog from a vehicle; ( 2 ) enter a public place without losing control of the dog; ( 3 ) to recover the leash if accidently dropped, and ( 4 ) to cope calmly with an access problem if an employee or customer questions the individual's right to bring a dog into that establishment.

B. The dog's ability to:

( 1 ) safely cross a parking lot, halt for traffic, and ignore distractions; ( 2 ) heel through narrow aisles; ( 3 ) hold a Sit-Stay when a shopping cart passes by or when a person stops to chat and pets the dog; (4 ) hold a Down Stay when a child approaches and asks to briefly pets the canine; ( 5 ) hold a Sit Stay when someone drops food on the floor; hold a Down Stay when someone sets a plate of food on the floor within 18" of the dog, then removes it a minute later. [The handler may say "Leave It" to help the dog resist the temptation.] ( 6 ) remain calm if someone else holds the leash while the handler moves 20 ft. away; ( 7 ) remain calm while another canine passes within 6 ft. of the team during the test. This can occur in a parking lot or store. Alternatively, you could arrange for a neighbor with a pet dog to stroll past your residence while you load your dog into a vehicle at the beginning of the test.

NOTE: Passing The Public Access Test officially "certifies" you to "register" your canine with Certified Registry. A professional canine trainer giving the test will provide the desired credentialing.

## CERTIFICATION:

Many states lack programs willing to certify dogs that did not go through that program's training course. The DOJ decided to foster "an *honor system,*" by making the tasks the dog is trained to perform on command rather than certification ID from specific programs, the primary way to differentiate between a service animal and a pet.

## DEFINITIONS

### What is a Task?

A task is a certain desired behavior or set of behaviors the dog is trained to habitually perform in response to a command or a particular situation such as the onset of a seizure, which cues the dog to perform a task. The task must be related to your disabling condition, helping you in some way.

### What is meant by "individually trained"?

A canine has been "individually trained" to do work or perform tasks for the benefit of a disabled individual when the canine is deliberately taught to exhibit the desired behavior or sequence of behaviors by rewarding the canine for the right response(s) and communicating, if only through silence, when the dog has made the wrong response in a particular situation.

A task is learned when the dog reliably exhibits the desired behavior whenever needed to assist his/her partner on command or cue. An example of work that is individually trained would be that performed by a guide dog, who takes directional commands, goes around obstacles in the team's path, halts to indicate a curb or some other change in elevation and refuses the "Forward" command in specific situations that would result in injury, such as an automobile entering the team's path. Examples of individually trained tasks include retrieving a phone, providing deep pressure therapy during a panic attack or providing balance support on a staircase to prevent a fall.

## What is NOT an individually trained task?

Spontaneous behavior a canine occasionally exhibits such as licking someone's face or barking does not qualify as a "trained task" under ADA even if it accidentally or coincidentally has a beneficial result. While everyone enjoys the emotional, social and safety benefits that a canine's presence can provide, those benefits do not constitute trained tasks that would transform a disabled person's pet into a legitimate Service Animal.

Why are individually trained Tasks so important?

Trained tasks that mitigate the effects of a disabling condition are the legal basis for granting access rights to disabled handlers under the Americans with Disabilities Act. An assistance dog with this special training is viewed as assistive technology / medical equipment, not as a pet. Businesses have the right to ask a disabled person, "What Tasks does your service animal perform?" Without a demonstration required.

This question can be posed if there is any doubt about the canine's legal status and whether to impose their restrictive pet policies. An acceptable answer might be, "my service dog is trained to provide me comfort when I am having anxiety"

Businesses also have the right to exclude any animal, including a service animal, who threatens the health or safety of other people through aggressive or unruly behavior. An assistance animal can also be evicted for disruptive behavior that interferes with a business providing goods or services. For example of a dog barking in a movie theater.

Below you will find a Training Log along with directions for filling it out. It is recommended that you keep a record of the hours you spend working (training) your canine both in your home and in public. Make Copies of the training log and record your work both with and without your trainer.

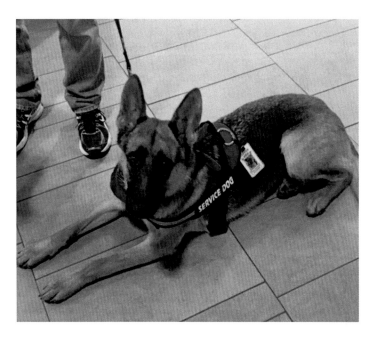

# TRAINING LOG

**(Owner's responsibility to keep records of specific trainings sessions and homework log)**

Date:

Owner Trainer's Name:

Dog's Name:

Breed:

Gender:

Age:

Week of: _____Hours (on Site) + (Outings)

Health:

Problems:

Outings:

Socialization:

Obedience:

Service Dog Tasks:

Manners:

Comments:

# How to Fill Out Your Training Log

Date:  Current date

Owner Trainer's Name:

Dog's Name:

Source: Rescue? Breeder?

Breed or Mix:

Gender:

Age:

Week of: <u>May 2 - 8, 2016 - 8 hrs.</u> Total Hours (<u>3.5 hrs.</u> on Site) + (<u>4.5 hrs.</u> Outings)

**Health:** Make a note if you gave Heartworm Preventative this week and /or used monthly flea control like Advantage or changed Flea & Tick collar. Make other notes, such as "treated ear infection." Anal gland scooting....had vet empty? Did you change diet? Progress on new diet or digestive upsets? Treated hot spot? Trimmed nails? Blowing coat? Improved on car sickness?

**Problems:** Are there any particular problems distressing you? Has there been improvement on any of the problems mentioned in previous logs? (e.g. Barking at other dogs, becoming over excited in the presence of other animals or fearful of getting into the back seat of the car, or refuses to eliminate outside of his backyard or won't use other footing except grass, etc.)

Outings:

1 Hour Mon. Canine Good Citizen (CGC) class, Trainers (instructor's name)
45 min. Tues. Bank - inside w/permission, parking lot work too; Trainer - (yr. name)
1 hr. 15 min. Thurs. PetSmart; Trainers - ( your name, assistant's name)
1 ½ hr. Saturday PetSmart, more work on dog distraction issue, Trainer - ( your name)

**Socialization:**

What novel sights, sounds, smells, taste or touch, footing, was the dog exposed to in an urban, suburban or rural environment in different kinds of weather? (E.g. a band in a park, a parade, a mounted policeman, Little League game, strangers in ethnic garb, eliminating in street near curb?) Did the dog improve when exposed to something that caused signs of stress earlier, such as an elevator ride, dog barking at him from behind a fence, working near an escalator, climbing a staircase or when asked to eliminate on different types of ground? What needs more work? (E.g. walking near heavy traffic, motorcycle revving up, garbage truck, approaching a mirror, screaming kids on schoolyard playground, holding a Sit Stay during a thunderstorm, etc.)

Obedience:

Where did you practice basic commands? (E.g. house, garage, neighborhood, outside shopping center). Any progress? What needs improvement? (E.g. out of sight Stays or Heel w/halt instead of Sit for balance or wheelchair work.) Practice Public Access Test exercises....holding Sit or Down when adult or child pets the dog or someone drops food on the floor or puts plate down by dog or passes with a shopping cart. Practice Stay or Come with a dropped leash indoors, outdoors in safe area. Have assistant tease dog at a distance with food, smooching, say "Hi, puppy, puppy" or bounce a ball while you keep him focused on you in a Sit or Down Stay. Advanced - practice Stay in public rest room, under table in restaurant, in stores in sight, you out of sight around a corner. Off leash heeling, Downs, recall indoors, outdoors in safe fenced area.

**Service Dog Tasks:**
What did you introduce this week? What progress has dog made on various tasks, like fetch the phone? Beginner, intermediate or advanced stage? Any setback? Where did you practice?

Manners:
Which manners were a priority this week? What improved? What needs more work? For example: Say please [with Sit Stay] for Supper, for Exiting house....expanded from 30 seconds to one minute! Enter, exit, riding in a car - improved. Lie quietly on side for nail grinder, grooming - needs work! Watchdog suppression - needs work! Jumping on visitors - needs work. Honor system - respecting "Leave It" edict re: bowl of treats on end table, 24/7....3rd week, also leaves bowl of treats on kitchen counter alone! Paw on knee - rarely tries this dominance behavior anymore. Licking self in public - only needed one correction this week, an "uh uh" with my disapproving glare at him. Doesn't do it at church anymore or in grocery store. No sniffing other dogs while "on duty" at obedience class or in neighborhood - needs more work.

Comments:
Anything unusual, worrisome, cute, exceptional? Did you read a book, see a video that helped with training? Reason for not practicing this week (e.g. sick, injured, family funeral, or dog neutered and must be kept very quiet for two weeks? etc.) Overall progress....fair? Good?

## Donna Marie Casey
## Professional Canine Trainer

# WORKING (3 ) SERVICE ANIMALS IN A LOCAL MALL

# Know the Different

# Types

# Of

# Service Animals

**Choose the right type of service animal to suit your lifestyle**

*"Bailey Makes a GREAT Service Animal"*

**Three Types of Service Dogs**

# 1 - SERVICE ANIMAL

<u>Service animal</u> help with performing a function for a person that is limited by a disability. A partial list of coverages: Mobility issues, visual impairment (blindness), hearing impairment (deafness), seizures, diabetes, PTSD, autism, epilepsy, multiple sclerosis (MS), and other physical/mental disabilities. Service dogs are covered by The Americans with Disabilities Act (ADA). Any breed of dog is acceptable. A Service Animal may fly in an airplane without charges associated. In addition, they are allowed in all housing regardless of pet policy & are protected in <u>All</u> <u>50</u> <u>States</u>

# 2 - EMOTIONAL SUPPORT ANIMAL

<u>Emotional support animal</u> help individuals with emotional problems by providing comfort and support. A Partial list of coverages: Anxiety, depression, bipolar/mood disorders, panic attacks, and other emotional/psychological conditions. Laws protecting this type of service animal Fair Housing Amendments Act & Air Carrier Access Act. Any breed of dog is acceptable. An Emotional Support Animal may fly in an airplane without any additional charges associated. They are allowed in all housing regardless of pet policy & are protected in <u>All</u> <u>50</u> <u>States</u>

# 3 - THERAPY DOG

Therapy dogs provide affection and comfort to individuals in hospitals, nursing homes, and other facilities. A Therapy animal <u>may not</u> fly on an airplane without additional charges associated and is <u>not covered</u> by Fair Housing Amendments Act & Air Carrier Access Act. They also are <u>not</u> <u>covered</u> in <u>all</u> <u>50</u> <u>States</u>.

# Public Service Access Test Requirements

**The Public Access Service test may take up to 2 hours
Depending on your type of service training
& the Type of Service Canine you choose**

## Sample Public Access Test  Requirements

**Controlled Approach:**                                    Pass    Fail
Navigating from your vehicle through the parking lot

**Controlled Entrance:**                                    Pass    Fail
Through Door-Way
Service Animal: Stop – Look

**Stairs:**                                                 Pass    Fail
No Pulling or Hesitation
Must Stay in line with Handler

**Stop & Recall:**                                          Pass    Fail
Service Animal in Sit or Down Stay: Drop Lead – Call to come

**Lead Drop:**                                              Pass    Fail
Handler Drops Lead **while in motion**
Service Animal must acknowledge lead drop & cannot stray

**Public Obedience:**                                       Pass    Fail
Sit, Down, Stay etc. while people are passing/watching

**Distraction with Children:**                              Pass    Fail
No Straying (children running, crying, laughing/strollers)

**Sample – Public Access Test**

| | Pass | Fail |
|---|---|---|

**Shopping Cart Passing:**        Pass   Fail
Cart passing very close, Service Animal does
Not move away from handler. (May be standing,
Sitting, Continue Heeling etc.)

**Heel with Shopping Cart:**        Pass   Fail
Loose lead, no pulling or straying

**Lead taken by Another Person/Handler:**    Pass   Fail
     Service Animal Remains Calm, May be
     Standing, sitting, looking for handler however
     Not pulling to get to original handler

**Command: Close or Visit**        Pass   Fail
     Service animal remains close, head on lap, while
     Ignoring passer byes (Praise & Affection ok)

**Navigating Tight Aisles/Spaces:**      Pass   Fail
     Service animal cannot hesitate, may look to
     Handler for direction, commands ok

**Food Distraction & Obedience:**      Pass   Fail
     People walking by with food
     Handler walking by people with food

**Purchasing Food:**        Pass   Fail
     Handler purchase food while service
     Animal remains on heel – little to no excitement (Sit, standing ok)

**Restaurant Handling @ Table:**      Pass   Fail
     Service Animal must sit close (not blocking aisles) & remain
     Under table or alongside ok

**Sample – Public Access Test**

**Food Distractions & Obedience:**                          Pass    Fail

     Food Drop - Service animal must "leave it"

     Beverage Drop - Service animal must "leave it"

     Waiter or Waitress – Interruptions (must remain in position non-reactive)

**Other Distractions:**                          Pass    Fail

     a) Other dogs/animals (entering, passing leaving)

     Service dog must remain non-reactive (acknowledgement ok

     No barking and/or growling etc.)

     b) Loud People/Children

     c) Person or persons at table leaving table & returning

        Little to no excitement

     d) Loud banging such as chair dropping etc.

**Elevator:**                          Pass    Fail

     a) Calm Entry

     b) Service Animal remain by handler

     c) Calm Exit

**Controlled Exit from Building:**                          Pass    Fail

**Controlled Loading into Vehicle:**                          Pass    Fail

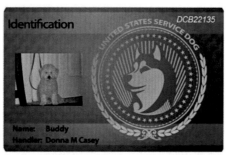

**"Buddy – Service Aninal Certifed to work with ADHD Children & Children on the Autistic Spectrum"**

**For Additional Information Regarding**
**FaceTime Consultations or Training Sessions**

# TEXT

**Donna Marie Casey**

# (516)368-5432

**Contact Information Required:**

- **Full Name**
- **Availability (avail. time to call or facetime)**
- **Canine Breed**
- **Brief description of Canine Training desired**